# AN ARABIAN ADVENTURE

# AN ARABIAN ADVENTURE

## A Dream Achieved

*Gifford S. Rossi*

*KEGAN PAUL INTERNATIONAL*
*London and New York*

First published in 1995 by
Kegan Paul International
UK: P.O. Box 256, London WC1B 3SW, England
Tel: (0171) 580 5511   Fax: (0171) 436 0899
E-mail: books@keganpau.demon.co.uk
Internet: http://www.demon.co.uk/keganpaul/
USA: 562 West 113th Street, New York, NY 10025, USA
Tel: (212) 666 1000   Fax: (212) 316 3100

Distributed by

John Wiley & Sons Ltd
Southern Cross Trading Estate
1 Oldlands Way, Bognor Regis
West Sussex, PO 22 9SA, England
Tel: (01243) 779 777   Fax: (01243) 820 250

Columbia University Press
562 West 113th Street
New York, NY 10025, USA
Tel: (212) 666 1000   Fax: (212) 316 3100

Set in Baskerville
by Intype, London
Printed in Great Britain by
TJ Press Ltd, Padstow, Cornwall

**British Library Cataloguing in Publication Data**
Rossi, Gifford S.
  Arabian Adventure: Dream Achieved
  I. Title
  338.7623820092

  ISBN 0–7103–0527–3

**US Library of Congress Cataloging in Publication Data**
Applied for

# CONTENTS

# LIST OF PLATES

# FOREWORD

This book is published posthumously at my husband's request. Gifford S. Rossi died on 7 August 1994 and I undertook the task to fulfil his wish, reliving what he once described as 'the most exciting adventure of our life'.

There are passages here that for some readers will be difficult to follow owing to the complexity of the 'deal', but I hope that, on the whole, it will succeed in presenting a moment that was interesting and captivating in the history of our relationship with the Arab world.

I would like to extend my thanks to all the Arab friends and associates who were of great help in the realization of what, at times, seemed almost an impossible project: (in alphabetical order) The Amir of Bahrain, His Highness Sheikh Isa Bin Sulman Al Khalifa; His Excellency Sheikh Khalifa bin Sulman Al-Khalifa; His Excellency Mr. Yousuf Al-Shirawi, His Excellency Dr. Abdulhady H. Taher; His Excellency Sheikh Ahmed Zaki Yamani.

I am especially indebted to Jack Hartshorn, Gifford's oldest and most constant friend, for assisting and encouraging me at the moment that was the most difficult and saddest of my whole life.

I must acknowledge with gratitude Sylvia Cape, our secretary for many years, for having been immensely helpful and without whose patience this book would not have been possible.

My thanks also go to Peter Hopkins of Kegan Paul International, who was so positively receptive from the beginning.

Marcella Rossi
February 1995

To Marcella
without whose love, encouragement,
partnership and loyalty this dream may have
never come true

# INTRODUCTION

In June 1967 the Arab/Israeli war succeeded in closing the Suez Canal in such a devastating way that many experts were predicting that it would never reopen. It was blocked by sunken ships, crumbled banks, dozens of tanks and a good deal of bad feeling on both sides. The oil industry had an unobstructed run to Japan from the Persian Gulf, but insufficient ships to deliver all the oil required by Western consumers. This was due to the fact that tankers of up to 65,000 dead-weight tonnage (DWT), which heretofore had been transitting the Suez Canal to the Persian Gulf, now had to make the much longer voyage around the Cape of Good Hope to collect and deliver oil to Europe and the Western Hemisphere. Many more ships were needed to deliver the same quantity of oil over a much greater distance. What added to the shortfall was that the demand for oil was increasing as industry converted to oil from coal-fired furnaces and boilers. The demand for petrol was also increasing, with more and more motor cars on the road.

The ever-resourceful ship-owning community found a solution – a much larger tanker, highly automated, requiring the same number of crew, which could carry three to four times more oil around the Cape than the older, smaller ships. Other operating costs pro rata per barrel of oil would be less than for the smaller ships. If the Suez Canal was ever reopened, they would be too big to pass through it. Nevertheless, they would be able to transport a barrel of oil more economically, even by the longer route, than any vessel able to transit the Canal.

The Canal had a record of disrupting the shipping and oil markets, being closed by war twice during a twelve-year period. These big, new ships would make the oil industry completely independent of the Suez Canal. Their size would be 200,000 DWT and upwards, and the class of vessel would be known as VLCCs (very large crude carriers).

Shipyards world-wide were not busy and shipowners rushed to place orders for the big new class of vessel. By 1968 the first VLCCs began to appear, and in 1969 there were about 60 of these giants in service. It was rumoured that Japan was gearing itself to produce about 40 VLCCs per year, and the shipping market was forecasting that a balance would be achieved between shipping capacity and oil demand when 700 VLCCs would be in service, possibly by 1974. Many adjustments had to be made at loading terminals and discharge ports to accommodate the big ships. Another problem of which the shipping press commented was that there were far too few dry docks to service this size vessel, and absolutely none between South-west Europe and Japan. Then disaster struck. Three VLCCs suffered major damage from explosion during one month in 1969.

On 12 December the *Marpessa*, a 206,805 DWT tanker owned by the Shell Group, sunk on her second voyage from damage caused by an explosion.

On 29 December the *Mactra*, over 200,000 DWT and also Shell owned, survived an explosion and was towed into Durban for partial repairs alongside as no dry dock of sufficient size existed. A 500–foot gash was torn in the vessel's hull and two crew members were killed. It was estimated at the time that 700 tons of steel would be required to strengthen her for towage to repair in Europe.

On 30 December the *King Haakon VII*, a Norwegian vessel, suffered an explosion off Liberia. She was also a VLCC of over 200,000 DWT. Eventually she was towed to Lisnave in Portugal for repairs and was redelivered to her owners in November 1970, eleven months later.

Towing these vessels to a shipyard large enough to accept them for repair was cripplingly expensive. It was against this background that I began to promote the building of a dry dock and repair yard for VLCCs in the Arabian Gulf (as the Arabs referred to it instead of the more commonly used Persian Gulf). The timing was not only right for a dry dock, but it also suited me, as it found me free to pursue the concept. I had recently sold my liquefied petroleum gas business, Northern LP-Gas Limited (NLPG) to ICI and the Northern Gas Board. My wife, Marcella, and I lived in a spacious flat in London with a large study which conveniently became my office. Sylvia Cape, my secretary from NLPG, remained in the north, but it was found that we worked very well by telephone. Letters and memoranda dictated that way arrived the next morning at home ready for me to sign and post. This arrangement with Sylvia happily continued for almost 30 years.

A dry dock might be called a hole in the water. It is like a very large swimming pool, with a pair of massive gates at the end facing open water. Before a vessel enters dock, the gates have been opened and the dock flooded. Once a ship is moored at the front of the dock, the gates are then closed and huge pumps start to empty the dock. After a few hours the hull is resting on blocks at the bottom of a completely dry dock, and it can be scraped free of marine growth, painted, the propeller and tail-shaft inspected, valves opened, and whatever else is required.

An extensive investigation about building costs of large dry docks, and their operating costs, together with repair prices, was undertaken. This enabled me to put together some preliminary cash flow estimates. I discovered that the first stage of Lisnave, located in Lisbon (the then newest and largest dry dock complex), had cost $40 million to build. It was suggested that a similar facility somewhere on the east coast of the Arabian Peninsular, where it was needed, would cost about two and a half times that figure. I soon came to the conclusion that revenue derived from competitive repair prices would never be able to amortize the construction cost. In other words, an Arabian Gulf VLCC yard would not be commercially viable no matter how badly it was needed. This was not daunting because, in any case, commercial investors would be very hard to find for a $100 million project in that part of the world. It was clear that it had to be approached from the aspect of creating a national prestige facility. Saudi Arabia, a leading producer whose oil had to be transported in VLCCs in order to reach the market place economically, should have an incentive in creating a VLCC dry dock in order to provide an 'on the spot' technical training school where young Arab Nationals could learn heavy engineering skills.

It was on that concept that I prepared a memorandum outlining the validity of a VLCC dry dock situated in the Arabian Gulf, and some of the benefits, such as technological transfer, which might accrue to an Arab oil producer from providing such a VLCC facility. I discussed the idea with an old friend, Jack Hartshorn, a very well known oil consultant and a personal acquaintance of Sheikh Ahmed Zaki Yamani. Sheikh Yamani, with his Western education and vision for his country to enter the modern world, seemed the person to interest in the dry dock. Jack is very much a pragmatist and I did not convince him of my idea at our first meeting on the subject of the dry dock. There were at least four more meetings with Jack until he finally told me to prepare a memorandum, as concise as possible, and he would see that Sheikh Yamani received it. 'It is just conceivable that the dry dock proposal might interest Saudi Arabia', he remarked.

The memorandum was given to Jack, who read it without comment, except to observe that it was a good thing I had not made it too long. I felt that a chain of events had been launched, and believed it would lead to Sheikh Yamani and that the dry dock would appeal to him. I did not anticipate what a path lay ahead of me. What follows is an account of the consequences of this memorandum over the next ten years.

# 1

# JANUARY – AUGUST 1969

In January 1969, Jack Hartshorn telephoned me to say that there had been an indication of interest in the dry dock memorandum. He said that early next month someone from Petromin, the Saudi National Oil Company, would be in London and perhaps a meeting could be arranged. This was great news. I busied myself polishing my presentation of the beneficial aspects of the dry dock and what I considered Saudi Arabia should find of interest.

At the beginning of February Jack telephoned to arrange a meeting with Maurice Brunel, Consultant to Petromin. We met in a suite at the London Hilton. Maurice Brunel is a Frenchman, with a long and interesting background in the oil industry, previously heading the Shell Company in Indo China. He had worked for Petromin the previous five years and lived in Riyadh. His special advice was related to down-stream operations which started with crude oil and converted it into the various products an oil company marketed – petrol, fertilizers, lube oil, LP-gas, petrochemicals, etc. We talked for over an hour, and Maurice said he would recommend the project for His Excellency the Minister's consideration.

Joyously I left the Hilton and felt we had made a start. I very much hoped that I would have the opportunity of meeting with Sheikh Yamani so that I could personally try to 'sell' the dry dock idea which was gaining momentum all the time.

A couple of weeks later Jack telephoned to say that Sheikh Yamani would like to see me at the Carlton Tower on 27 February at 17:00. Jack and I met in the lobby just before the appointed hour and the hall porter telephoned the Minister's suite to say that we were downstairs. Shortly afterwards, a young man in Western clothes, but wearing the traditional Saudi goatee and moustache came up to us. Jack introduced me to Hisham Ali Reza, the Deputy Governor of Petromin. He was a very personable chap who, of course, spoke flawless English. I asked him if he was a relation to the Ali Reza who had brought the holy water from Saudi Arabia at the launching of the Onassis tanker *Al Malik Saud Al Awal* in 1953. He said that had been his father. I mentioned that I had

5

met him as I was at the launch which took place in Hamburg. I was at the time Managing Director for Niarchos (Hamburg) GmbH. Actually, he looked very much like his father, with an intelligent face and a great dignity of bearing. We went up to Sheikh Yamani's suite, in which six young Saudis were sitting. Ali Reza introduced us, Jack knew them all. Nothing much was said, except an offer of tea or coffee, which we knew better than to decline. Afterwards there was silence and I felt the scrutiny of piercing Arab eyes trying to determine if I was up to some con game. Finally, the waiter arrived and we all occupied ourselves with the cup and saucer we were holding. Time passed slowly, but eventually the door opened and Sheikh Yamani walked in holding a small dog. He shook hands and greeted me in the courtly way of the statesman which he is. His manner was a combination of austerity, dignity, and gentle welcome; I shall never forget my first meeting with that charismatic man. He sat cuddling a mink coloured Pomeranian in his lap, and listened while I explained the dry dock proposal. He kept quiet and stared at me, as if trying to read beyond what I was saying. When I finished, he asked whether I had an estimate of cost and how long it would take to build; I did not know the answer to either question. He requested me to prepare a feasibility study for him to consider. I said I would, thanked him and departed.

Afterwards many questions occurred to me, the answers to which I felt were important to the input of the feasibility study. I telephoned him at the Carlton Tower the next day, hoping for a second meeting, and was told that he had gone down to Sutton Place to spend the day with the multi-millionaire John Paul Getty. He left England immediately after, so I had to proceed with the study on my own assumptions.

I wanted a visual lay-out of what the dry dock complex would look like to include in my study, which I knew would have too many words and numbers to make interesting reading. A plan, or schematic drawing, would not be enough. What was wanted was an artist's impression, complete with palm trees. I could see considerable costs being incurred in putting together the material, with nothing tangible apart from Sheikh Yamani's request for a study. I was so convinced of the suitability of the project that I decided I would take the risk of supporting the costs involved.

I went to Spain to see an old friend, a shipowner in Bilbao, who was Chairman of the shipping company Naviera Vizcaina. This was Don Fernando de Azqueta. He had previously told me of a Spanish engineering company, SENER, which was operated by a brilliant scientist, Manual Sendagorta, who had worked with Werner von Braun on the American space programme. Returning to Spain, Sendagorta had formed a company which specialised in maritime construction, breakwaters, dry docks, harbours and dams. A meeting was arranged. I told Sendagorta of the feasibility study I had been asked to prepare by Sheikh Yamani. I invited SENER to participate in it to provide initial design, estimate of cost and building time, and above all, an attractive comprehensible picture of what it would look like when it was finished. I would provide estimates of labour costs and other operating overheads, as well as an estimate of the number of ships to be docked and repair revenue in order to project a cash flow. Manuel Sandegorta agreed, and thus began our intense joint effort with fortnightly flights to Spain.

I was still working as a consultant for NLPG and my visits to Newcastle to attend at NLPG were extremely useful. There was a lot of paperwork beginning to accumulate for the dry dock study and Sylvia was invaluable. There were such office machines as photocopiers, calculators, etc., which I did not have in my study in London. Work progressed and an excellent drawing of the dry dock complex had been made in Spain.

On 14 May Hisham Ali Reza, Jack Hartshorn and I met in London. I showed them the draft of the feasibility study and the coloured drawing of the dry dock. Hisham Ali Reza said that he was returning to the Kingdom (all Saudis referred to their country as the Kingdom) and would show it to His Excellency Dr. Abdulhady Taher, the Governor of Petromin. I would not part with the draft study, explaining that I was still waiting for some input before the calculations could be completed, but I gave him a colour photograph of the dry dock drawing.

On 19 May I received a cable from Dr. Taher confirming interest in the dry dock project. Another step forward on that very long road. On 28 May I had my second meeting with Sheikh Yamani in London. I showed him the feasibility study and gave him a copy. It was very encouraging to find him still interested personally in the project and this time he asked a number of informed questions, showing that he had been talking with others about the project. I assumed he had asked ARAMCO (Arabian American Oil Company, comprising Exxon, Texaco, Chevron and Mobil), the concessionaires for oil production in Saudi Arabia, for their opinion of an Arabian Gulf VLCC dry dock. He asked the vital question, who would operate the dry dock as there was certainly no indigenous skill of that type in the Kingdom? A great deal of thought and discussion had taken place concerning that matter over the past year, and I was able to answer Sheikh Yamani's question. I explained it would be necessary to make a long-term, say ten-year, management contract with a well-known ship-repairer who would provide all management services and workforce down to unskilled labour, until over the contract period all of the jobs could be carried out by Saudi Nationals. One of the duties of the management company would be to establish a training school. This appeared to spark new thinking and interest on the part of Sheikh Yamani. He asked me if I could find suitable managers with a workforce able to come to the Arabian Gulf. My answer was an incautious affirmative. Sheikh Yamani

7

said he would discuss it when he got back to the Kingdom. He said he would be in Vienna for an OPEC Meeting on 3 July and requested me to meet him there. In the mean time he asked me to think of some shipyard which might be interested in the management role. This time there was recognizable progress, but I also became aware that soon I might have to prove that an operator could be found and I began to review in my mind all the shipyards I knew and which ones might be suitable and willing to send more than 1,000 men out to the Arabian Gulf.

On 5 July following the OPEC Meeting, Jack Hartshorn and I met Sheikh Yamani in his suite at the Hotel Imperial in Vienna. With him was Dr. Taher. Dr. Taher was altogether different from Sheikh Yamani. He spoke, acted and resembled an American. He has been aptly called a 'ball of fire'. His was a very pragmatic pugnacious personality. He came straight to the point and didn't mind being offensive; there was none of the diplomacy of the Minister, but as with Sheikh Yamani, I took an immediate liking to him. Sheikh Yamani asked me to outline the project to Dr. Taher. When I finished he asked, 'Where do you come in?' This was a question for which I was honestly unprepared. I hadn't thought that far forward. I could only reply, 'I don't know yet.' Sheikh Yamani said that I should come to Saudi Arabia to investigate whether there was a suitable place to locate the dock. He told me to cable him in Taif after I knew the date of my arrival. He explained that the Government moved to Taif in the summer because temperatures in Riyadh, the capital, became unbearable. Taif was at an altitude of 1,500 metres above sea level. I returned to London aware that I was becoming deeply involved and hopeful that I would be able to perform on such unfamiliar terrain.

On my return to London it became very necessary to meet with SENER in Spain before my trip to Saudi Arabia. I had to learn as much as possible about the problems of building a dry dock on an Arabian Gulf shore. I anticipated being confronted by experts when I got to Saudi Arabia. Sheikh Yamani had suggested that I arrive in Taif during the last half of August, when he was certain to be there. Happily this left me more than a month to prepare my information.

In Spain Fernando Azqueta disclosed some of the new problems shipowners were experiencing in operating VLCCs. He said that his company had ordered two such ships from AESA (Astilleros Española SA), the Spanish nationalized group of shipbuilders. I asked Fernando if AESA did any repairs in their newbuilding dock and was informed that it would be very unprofitable for them as it would interfere with their building programme. It took 5–6 months to build a VLCC hull, and as soon as it was floated out, the keel plates for the next hull would be laid down, thus enabling the yard to produce two VLCCs per year. They could not afford to interrupt the programme and tie up the dock for 8–10 days to repair a ship in it.

As well as Fernando, other people in Spain were extremely co-operative. Spain produced no oil, nor did it have concessions in oil-producing countries. The fact that my investigation appeared to be on behalf of Saudi Arabia excited them very much as they hoped it might lead to a direct oil contract, thus by-passing the major oil companies. Talk of oil was avoided and skirted whenever it was frequently raised; I only said that if this project was realized and Spain was involved, they would certainly have the opportunity to meet with Petromin and have the chance to discuss oil. In all fairness, their help was given with no strings attached, and they painstakingly explained to a layman the problem of constructing a dry dock. After finding a site which gave on to water of at least 75 foot depth, preferably with no silting, borings would have to be taken to determine the resistance of the bottom because it would have to support a large concrete pool which would be filled with water frequently, and when it was empty would have to support a VLCC which would be resting on blocks at the bottom of the empty pool. They explained about the necessity of infrastructure, such as roads, electricity, etc. Notes were taken and I felt much better informed than when I had met Sheikh Yamani in Vienna, but I greatly feared that none of the ideal conditions described would be found in Saudi Arabia.

I returned to London and was keen to apply for my Saudi Arabian visa which I had been told sometimes took two to three weeks. My travel agent sent me a visa application form and amongst the usual information and photograph requested was a certificate of religion. I understood the reason, but wondered how I could prove I was a Christian as I did not attend Church regularly. I went to the American Embassy for help, but it was explained they never got involved in religious matters.

There was a very pleasant church – Holy Trinity, Brompton – which I passed frequently as it provided a short-cut to Hyde Park where I went for my early morning walk. I called in, met the Vicar, the Reverend Nicolas Rivett-Carnac, and explained my problem. He asked me if I was a Christian and I replied in the affirmative. He then sat down and wrote out a statement on Holy Trinity letterhead that I was known to him and was a Christian. This was all I needed to complete my visa application.

Nicolas and I became friends over the years and I regularly attended services at Holy Trinity. He came from a Naval family and after leaving school had worked in the city for a firm of shipbrokers, Clarksons, that I knew well. He had found that sort of work did not offer him enough motivation and he became ordained as a Minister of the Church. He was very committed to helping the lost young people, particularly the drug addicted. He has subsequently opened a mission in the East end of London where he now devotes all of his time.

After several visits to the visa section of the Saudi Embassy, my visa was ready, and I cabled Sheikh Yamani that I would arrive in Jeddah on 25 August.

# 2

# AUGUST 1969

Aboard a BOAC (British Overseas Airways Corporation, now British Airways) VC10 heading for Jeddah that day in August 1969, I did not know what to expect. The last time I had been near the Arabian Peninsula was in 1946 when I had been an airline captain with KLM and we made a regular fuel stop in Bahrain *en route* to Djakarta (then named Batavia). I knew it would be very hot and humid and absolutely dry as far as alcoholic drinks were concerned. It was quite amusing as the stewardess appeared during the last hour of the seven hour flight and asked disembarking passengers for Jeddah if they would like a drink. She offered me a whisky and said, 'Last chance, you know'.

Jeddah airport at that time was relatively primitive, apart from the very long reinforced runways which a jet needed to take off in the hot summer months. When the cabin door was opened, we were assailed by a blast of hot humid air and could see a Pakistani man in sandals slowly pushing the steps up to the aircraft. He was in no hurry, it was much too hot to hurry. It was dark, about 19:30 local time. We had to walk at least 250 metres into the terminal building where we arrived drenched with sweat which was beginning to seep through our jackets. The building was not air-conditioned and the ten other passengers who had left the aircraft with me got in line behind the immigration desk. Our passports were slowly scrutinized, every page turned over in case an Israeli visa or immigration stamp was showing. As each page was turned, the official would lift his gaze from the document and stare at us with an accusatory glance. We were not Muslims and therefore suspect. At last we were all cleared and able to proceed to the customs hall to collect our luggage – but it hadn't arrived. At first I thought it had been left on the aircraft and would be sent back from Bombay; I looked through the window; the VC10 was still on the ground and I saw the same Pakistani crawl into the hold of the aircraft and hand down one suitcase at a time to his less efficient helper. The helper took the piece of luggage, walked half way to the terminal, put it down, and returned to the aircraft to receive another case from the man inside the hold. This went on until about

11

fifteen suitcases were piled half-way between the aircraft and the terminal building. At that point, the senior man arrived with a hand-cart on which his helper piled three pieces of luggage. After five trips, all the baggage was in the customs hall. Each suitcase was thoroughly searched by a white-robed customs officer in case anyone had been trying to smuggle alcoholic beverages. At last I retrieved my suitcase and made for the exit. It was then 21:05.

A young man in traditional dress stepped forward and, in impeccable English, introduced himself as Abdulla Gamma from Petromin. I said I hoped he had not been waiting long, to which he replied, 'Not at all, you came through quite quickly'. A Petromin car drove us to the Kanda-rah Palace Hotel, where a room had been booked. Abdulla Gamma told me he would call for me the following morning at 5:00 in order to take the 5:30 flight to Taif, and we said goodnight.

It was my first stay at the Kandarah, but I got to know it well; for years it was the best hotel in Jeddah and because it was so much better than the others it was very difficult to get a room unless Petromin or the Ministry of Petroleum booked it. In 1969 the great influx of every kind of Western and Eastern business man was just beginning. The avail-ability of hotel rooms caught up with the situation seven years later. Until then it was not uncommon to see senior Vice-Presidents of major banks, with shoes and jackets off, curled up on one of the sofas in the lobby, where they would spend the night hoping that on the following day the meeting they had come for would take place and not be postponed again. Most people in the lobby had large litre bottles of Soha mineral water to assuage their thirst during the night as all service stopped before mid-night. Up until 1978, the lobby of the hotel resembled the lounge of a busy airport during the holiday season – but there was hope of giant rewards for their patience.

I was ready for Mr. Gamma at 5:00 the following morning and we walked the short distance to the airport. There was no check-in desk; one showed a valid ticket at the barrier and then waited. Just before departure time the gate was opened and everyone ran for the front or rear door of the Saudi Airlines Douglas DC9. Sometimes there would not be a seat and one would be turned back to catch the next flight two hours later. When Abdulla Gamma said run, I ran, and we found two seats together. He explained he had proposed the first flight as it was easier to find a seat. We took off for Taif. I noticed that the map showed we made a detour so as not to fly over Mecca, which was *en route*. He explained that this was also the case with the road, to ensure that no non-Muslims enter or pass over Mecca, the most holy city in the Muslim world. It was a short flight and we arrived at Taif airport at 6:15. We took a taxi to the Messarrah Hotel. Abdulla said it was too early to go to the Ministry of Petroleum office so we had breakfast.

At 8:00 we walked the short distance from the hotel to the office of the Ministry of Petroleum, which was also shared with Petromin. There was a very marked difference between the temperature and humidity of Jeddah and Taif. Taif was sunny and dry with a temperature of about 18°C. I felt very exhilarated and didn't know whether it was due to the climate or to the fact that I would soon be meeting Sheikh Yamani to discuss the dry dock project.

Abdulla conducted me into the waiting room. A short time later I was shown into Sheikh Yamani's office. On our previous three meetings he had been dressed in Western clothes, but on that day he was wearing the spotless white robes native to the Kingdom. He smiled and welcomed me with his usual courtesy. Over the next few years I was to meet him often, and on each occasion I was impressed by what might be described as his extra dimension. There was at once a feeling of immense power, and at the same time, gentleness. He was naturally diplomatic and chose his words with a lawyer's gravity. His self-control was immense. One could not imagine him losing his temper, even in heated OPEC debate. I never heard him malign anyone, not even ministers of radical Arab countries with whom he was often in opposition over policy. Perhaps the single quality which emerged most strongly was his great depth. The intelligence observed through the expression of his eyes was based on a profound wisdom.

After we sat down, he handed me several maps – admiralty charts showing the Eastern coastline of Saudi Arabia and the shores of the Arabian Gulf. He asked me to look at them and in a little while he and Dr. Taher would have a further meeting with me. I studied the charts and was disappointed to find very shallow water near the coast, except at Dammam which, although deeper, was only about 26 foot. I was hoping to find at least 45–50 foot close on shore. There were few roads, except in the Dammam area.

Dr. Taher invited me into his office. He explained that the Minister (as Sheikh Yamani was called by his colleagues) had to attend the morning conference with the King (Faisal). Dr. Taher came immediately to the point and said that Petromin would like to engage my services as consultant on the dry dock project. We quickly agreed terms, and I was pleased at last to have an official sponsor which would make my dealings with third parties easier. We talked about the dry dock and whether I thought it would be financially viable. From the beginning I am pleased that I did not mislead on that point. I replied that the dry dock had many advantages, such as a source of training in engineering skills, an industrial venture with spin-off, a facility which would surely be used to capacity by shipowners, but the building cost would be at least double that of a dry dock in Europe or Japan, and expatriate labour on which the repair yard would depend in the initial years would also probably be double the cost of that in Europe or Japan because of overseas pay allowances, housing to be created, and even transportation out and repatriation every two years.

Dr. Taher said he had assumed that, but they still wished to proceed because the Minister and he recognized the dry dock as a logical step towards industrialization. Steel factories or automobile plants would be even greater loss leaders. I was relieved to hear this pragmatic approach in accepting that the dry dock would not be profitable.

Sheikh Yamani joined us and said that Prince Naif had invited him to lunch and Dr. Taher and I were included in the invitation. Sheikh Yamani led me to his car and introduced me to his three young children, Mai, Maha and Hanni. Mai was 11, Maha 9 and Hanni 7. We drove off, Sheikh Yamani at the wheel, and he pointed out the King's palace and various other sights as we left Taif heading for the open country. I was surprised how green the countryside was. Sheikh Yamani said that grapes, peaches and figs grew in abundance and we were going to have an outdoor lunch in a pomegranate grove. We drove down a lane into a field where there were two large tents and many cars parked. We walked to the first tent and took our shoes off. The ground was covered with carpets. Prince Naif greeted Sheikh Yamani and I was introduced to him. He was one of the sons of the founder of the country, Abdul Aziz ibn Saud, who had been King for 51 years. Prince Naif had his father's height, and the characteristic moustache and goatee, very black hair and eyes contrasting with pale skin. A fierce but smiling countenance. There were about 50 guests, all male except for Mai and Maha. We sat down on the carpets with our legs drawn up under us. We were served sweet mint tea and a variety of fruit juices. I can recommend the pomegranate juice for its remarkable flavour, tangy and not too sweet. Soon giant Sudanese passed among us, dipped our hands in a bowl of water and then dried them for us, with a clean unused towel for each guest. It soon became apparent there were no Saudis doing domestic jobs. There were no poor, the desert Bedouin was too proud to do menial work. Labour was imported from the Sudan for unskilled jobs – domestics, waiters, etc., and semi-skilled jobs, such as airport workers, were done by Pakistanis.

We followed our host into the next tent where, in the centre, was an immense feast of lamb, cooked vegetables, salads, fruits and various breads which had been arranged in a very decorous pattern. As at a buffet, everyone was handed a plate, but no knives and forks. We were seated in a circle around the tempting spread and reached forward with our right hand and took whatever appealed. The practice was to select a combination of ingredients from one's plate, roll them together with the fingers of the right hand, then transfer them to the mouth. It was a very light-hearted, happy occasion, with much laughter and animated conversation. At the right moment, the Sudanese appeared with large coffee pots and little cups, into which they poured cardamom coffee. They kept filling the small cup until it was turned upside down and one made as if to shake it. Suddenly, everybody got up, thanked their host, and began looking for their shoes, which had been left outside the tent. I retrieved mine and sat down in the field to put them on. However, I was unable to do so as I had no shoe horn. My feet were very long and narrow, and ready-made shoes do not usually fit me. I have my shoes made to measure and require a shoe horn to put them on. I walked across the grass stubble with my shoes in my hand to Sheikh Yamani's car and explained my problem. He thought it funny and reached into the back of the car for a briefcase, from which he produced a shoe horn which he handed to me. It was then 15:30. He said he was going home with the children and that as the next flight to Jeddah was not until 19:30 he had arranged for a car to drive me there. I thanked him and he said we would meet at his office the following day and drove off.

The drive down to Jeddah was interesting as the fertile plateau of Taif gradually turned to rocky scrub and then desert. The road had been built by an Italian construction company and finished fairly recently. It descended through a series of hairpin turns, not dissimilar from the St. Gotthard Pass. We came to a fork, with the right-hand being the road to Mecca and the left bypassing Mecca en route to Jeddah, which had been built for non-Muslims to use.

When I arrived at the Kandarah Palace, Abdulla Gamma was waiting for me. We had dinner together. Although he spoke excellent English, all his studies had taken place in the Kingdom. He had been to Europe a couple of times, and was hoping that Petromin would send him to America to study petroleum engineering. He told me that up to then there were no technical colleges in the Kingdom, and most young Saudis wanting an engineering education had to go abroad. After dinner he said goodnight, and informed me that he would come for me at 05:00 the following morning.

I went up to my room. It had been an interesting day of mixed pleasures and I had been appointed consultant to Petromin on the dry dock project. I felt a strange certainty that the dry dock would be built and that it was being pushed forward by forces other than myself. It was a moment of elation and I found it hard to sleep, which in any case would have been difficult as the air-conditioning was not working. Eventually it was time to get up and meet Abdulla. The same performance to board the aircraft, and again we were lucky and found two seats. This time we went straight to the offices of the Ministry where we sat down and were served coffee. We didn't wait long; at about 7:00 someone escorted me into Sheikh Yamani's office; he greeted me and told me that later we would be joined by some Aramco people to whom he wanted me to explain the dry dock project. He then excused himself as he had to attend the King at the palace. He said that the Aramco people were flying over from Dharhan and would arrive around 10:30. He suggested that I might find a walk through the souk interesting and Abdulla took me on a tour. Every Arab town or city has at least one souk, which is the general market with individual stalls selling everything from meat to wool of all colours, nuts, fruit, beaten brass ware, utensils of all kinds, swords, camel saddles, watches, cigarettes and perfume essence, etc. We bought and ate some fresh dates which were grown in Taif.

When we got back to the office, the Aramco people had arrived and were in with the Minister. I was sent for, and Sheikh Yamani introduced me to Frank Jungers, General Manager (later Chairman), and Dick Copeland, Technical Manager. I was asked to explain the dry dock concept. When I finished, Frank Jungers asked why a shipowner would want to dock his VLCC in the Arabian Gulf, except in an emergency, which didn't happen that frequently. Thanks to Don Fernando Azqueta, I had the answer. I explained that when a VLCC arrived in Europe and discharged its cargo, it would have to be gas free before a repair yard would accept it for dry docking. They could not risk a tanker which was not gas free being ignited by a spark from a metal tool setting off an explosion, not only damaging the tanker, but the dock itself. It took about seven days to gas free a VLCC. This meant that the vessel would be off-hire for seven days. Each day off-hire at the then prevailing charter rates cost a shipowner $20,000. Effectively he would have to add $140,000 to the docking and repair cost. Whereas, a VLCC on the ballast run from Europe or Japan would vent the tanks and arrive in the Arabian Gulf gas free and could enter dry dock without delay. Frank Jungers had spent a lot of time in Saudi Arabia and was not convinced, but Dick Copeland was more supportive. Aramco had been operating in Saudi Arabia since the 1930s and had created an entire infrastructure to support their 25,000 employees, who lived in a fully American town in the Eastern Province of Saudi Arabia at Dharhan. Aramco had built hospitals, schools, playing fields, cinemas, and everything that went with a small American town. The 25,000 people, apart from running the amenities, were mostly engaged in exploring, drilling and producing oil, and also refining it. Frank Jungers spoke from his knowledge of how difficult it was to get things done in the Kingdom, with its paucity of local labour. We discussed the project objectively for over an hour, until Sheikh Yamani announced that he had invited us all to lunch in the new house he was having built at Al-Hadda, outside of Taif. He said the Japanese Ambassador and his entourage would also be coming. On the way to the cars he told me he had sent Abdulla Gamma to the Kandarah in Jeddah to pack my bag and bring it to the airport. After lunch the Aramco aircraft would fly us to Kuwait where he had a meeting. Things happened at an interesting pace. Sheikh Yamani received the Japanese Ambassador in a large reception room of the partially completed house. We were about 12, Frank Jungers, Dick Copeland, Dr. Taher, the Japanese Ambassador, his six aides and myself. Fruit drinks were passed around. The Japanese Ambassador asked one of his team to give him a package which he unwrapped and then presented to Sheikh Yamani. It was the latest multi-band transistorised tape-deck, very compact. Sheikh Yamani expressed his sincere diplomatic pleasure. Then the Ambassador told him, 'Push please marked tape'. Sheikh Yamani did as he was told, and Arabic music blared forth. We all laughed in sympathy and admired this modern technocratic nation which equip their Ambassadors as super salesmen. Sheikh Yamani explained that the dining-room was not yet finished, so we would eat in a tent in the garden. He had the same enjoyable feast of many delicacies and a whole roast lamb, as I had experienced the day before.

After lunch Sheikh Yamani said goodbye to the Japanese. He took Frank Jungers in his car, and Dick Copeland and I followed in another. We drove to the airport, about half an hour's distance. Waiting on the tarmac by the Aramco aircraft was Abdulla Gamma with my suitcase. As far as I could observe, things worked very efficiently at the Ministry of Petroleum. We boarded the aircraft and took off for Kuwait, about an hour's flight. The Aramco Lear was very comfortable. During the flight Sheikh Yamani and Frank Jungers talked, and Dick Copeland provided me with very helpful information about the Saudi coast, water depths, etc. He then very kindly gave me a printed forecast of the incidence of traffic of vessels over 100,000 DWT to load at Aramco facilities in the Arabian Gulf on a monthly basis for the next five years. This was really a piece of privileged information, which formed a basis of many of the future calculations we were to make on the dry dock throughput.

We landed at Kuwait; Sheikh Yamani and I got out, the others remained on board and the aircraft immediately taxied away for take off. Waiting for Sheikh Yamani was Sheikh Abdul Rahman Al-Attiki, the Kuwait Minister of Petroleum and Abdul Aziz Al-Turki, the Deputy Secretary General of OAPEC (Organization of Arab Petroleum Exporting Countries). We got into two cars, the two Ministers together and Mr. Al-Turki and I following – with no immigration or customs formalities – straight from aircraft to car to road, which took us to the Kuwait Sheraton. On arrival Sheikh Yamani told me he would telephone my room later, some time after dinner. The Kuwait Sheraton was a very pleasant surprise, which I had not expected to find in the Arab world. It was fully air-conditioned and looked like all other Sheratons. It even had bacon and ham on the breakfast menu, but Kuwait, like Saudi Arabia, observed the non-alcoholic beverage rule. Mr. Al-Turki had joined the two Ministers, so I dined early and then went up to my room and made some notes. At this stage I was more aware of obstacles to building the dry dock than I was at having made progress.

At about 23:00 Sheikh Yamani telephoned me and asked me to come up to his apartment. He kept a permanent suite at the hotel, and he showed me the elaborate radio telephone system which enabled him to communicate at any time with the Kingdom. The ordinary telephone link between the two countries had not yet been established. The satellite station was still five years away. He told me that he had caused OAPEC to be formed in 1967, and he was asked to become its first Secretary General. He felt the dry dock project was something for OAPEC, and would be its first industrial venture. He said he had discussed this with the Kuwait Minister of Petroleum and the OAPEC Deputy Secretary General. He suggested, and they had accepted, that Petromin would pursue the dry dock project on behalf of OAPEC. He had told them that Petromin had retained me as consultant to progress the dry dock. With that he said goodnight, and wished me a comfortable flight to London the next day.

I left Kuwait the following morning and was home in London by 16:00 with a lot to tell Marcella.

# 3

# AUGUST – DECEMBER 1969

On my return to London I began to collect information about those shipyards which might have the experience and interest in managing the dry dock/repair yard. The position of shipyard order books had changed from famine to feast since the 1967 closure of the Suez Canal. This was particularly true for the yards capable of building VLCCs. Shipowners were paying premiums to those builders who could give early delivery, i.e. within the next two years. In the whole of Europe there were only 14 shipyards capable of constructing this class of vessel (three in the UK, two in France, two in Germany, one in Italy, three in Sweden, one in Holland, one in Belgium and one in Spain).

It was a difficult selling job, with a credibility gap, to try and interest a busy shipyard to divert its attention to studying the management of a facility which was not yet certain to be built, and for which most details were missing. The holiday season, during which most industries in Spain closed (August) was almost over. I made an appointment for the following week with SENER in Bilbao. I reluctantly related the pessimism expressed by Frank Jungers about the difficulty of mounting an industrial project in Saudi Arabia; this was counteracted by the support which Sheikh Yamani, and through him, OAPEC, was giving to the proposal.

SENER pointed out that the Arabian Gulf had natural pluses as well as minuses. They explained that the most important single function of a dry dock, apart from cleaning the vessel's hull and bottom, was to paint it. Rain interfered with painting, and sometimes made it impossible; in Europe, many days work were lost to rain. They produced statistics for both North and South Europe. It was shown that for ten months of the year, the climate in the Arabian Gulf was perfect for painting, and only during the two very hot and humid months from mid-July to mid-September would there be difficulties. They, of course, were aware of the problem of shallow coastal water and expressed the view, subject to inspecting the site, that Dammam, adjacent to the Abdul Aziz Pier, could be suitable. Dredging would need to be carried out to create the necessary water depth, and the dry dock/repair yard could be built in close proximity to the pier, benefiting from some existing infrastructure, such as access roads, electric power, etc. It was agreed that they would expand on their preliminary study and then, early in 1970, they would send some engineers with me to visit the area. SENER did not consider the problems insurmountable and, of course, they were interested in engineering the dry dock/repair complex. They certainly had the know-how and were a group of very intelligent marine specialists.

I left for London and resumed the search for shipyards to manage the dry dock. It was logical to start with the three British VLCC yards, Harland & Wolf in Belfast, Upper Clyde in Glasgow, and Swan Hunter in Newcastle. I had acquaintances in all three.

The Belfast yard was the first approached, and they immediately declined. Upper Clyde Shipbuilders (UCS) was next on the list. UCS had been much in the press at that time. It was a grouping of all the famous old shipyards on the river Clyde, headed by an energetic Chairman, Tony Hepper, and a Managing Director with a powerful personality, Ken Douglas, who had the support of the Trade Unions. One of the newer yards in the grouping, Scott Lithgow, had VLCC capability. The other yards were specialists in the building of passenger liners and a variety of cargo ships, for which there was diminishing demand. Their main problem, which had taken up so much press comment, was due to a plan to reduce the labour force of the inefficient yards in the group and concentrate on expanding two of the efficient and more modern yards which specialised in ships for which there was a demand – the usual problem which was insoluble amicably, and which faced those long-established industries, such as steel, shipbuilding and coal. It seemed that a combination of VLCC experience and a surplus of labour made them a candidate for managing the dry dock. In an ideal situation one could imagine 1,500 men about to lose their jobs being very keen to get jobs at higher pay, leave the rain and cold of the river Clyde area and take their families to the sunny climate of the Arabian Gulf where they would not be bullied by union bosses and their wages would not be taxed. Unions are illegal in Saudi Arabia. Of course, we don't live in an ideal world, and although Tony Hepper and Ken Douglas were enthusiastic, there were many problems. The first to emerge was insurmountable – the workers loved their local pubs which to them made bearable their very hard life, working outdoors in freezing weather with their hands sticking to very cold steel and other inhumanities. It would be too much for them to face not only parting from their favourite pubs, but going to work in an alcohol-free country. Ken Douglas believed that of the 12,000 workers, 1,500 could be found who didn't feel that way and would welcome the opportunity of financial betterment for themselves and their families, so talks continued and Tony Hepper was keen to present the possibility to the Minister of Industry, Mr. Tony Benn. The UCS Sales Director, Admiral John Scotland, was a very helpful person who had commanded the British Naval Station in Bahrain. He knew the area well and believed that a VLCC repair yard with dry dock would do very well in the Arabian Gulf. He pointed out that the English had always got on well with Arab Nationals, and since English was the second language taught to young Arabs at school, he considered it beneficial to the secondary purpose of the dry dock to act as a technical training college to have a common language. Admiral Scotland believed in the validity of the scheme and provided staunch support within UCS.

Dr. Taher cabled that he would be in Brussels on 15 October and suggested that we meet. It was time to return to Bilbao and learn of progress on the design being adapted to Dammam. Marcella and I decided to go by car and to combine the meeting in Brussels with a visit to Bilbao where we had been invited to attend the launch of a ship belonging to Don Fernando Azqueta.

When Dr. Taher and I met, he handed me a contract in respect to my consultancy for Petromin. The details were precisely what we had agreed in Taif and we each signed the document. Dr. Taher then asked what progress had been made and I told him that UCS might possibly be interested in managing the dry dock. I explained what UCS was and suggested that their experience seemed to qualify them, particularly as one of the yards in the group was a VLCC builder. He said he had never dealt with shipbuilders, and would like to meet someone from UCS. He gave me a date in early November when he would be in Rome and asked me to meet him there with an executive of UCS.

The next morning we headed for France; the weather was beautiful all the way down and the following morning in Bilbao we saw Don Fernando's tanker launched, which was followed by a lunch for all the guests and speeches by various dignitaries. The afternoon was spent with SENER; they had made a model of the dry dock which also showed the Abdul Aziz Pier in Dammam. The pier was very long, extending from the desert shore, about a mile into deep water. It could berth and unload five cargo ships on each side of the pier and contained large warehouses. Neither SENER nor I had seen it, but all the necessary information was available from navigation manuals, one of which contained a large photograph. I disclosed my news about UCS and told them of my now official status with Petromin. At that particular moment both SENER and I anticipated quick progress towards realizing the Arabian Gulf dry dock. For identification within SENER it had even been given a name, the Arabian Gulf Repair Yard. The initials spelt AGRY and for a long time it was known as that.

The next morning we drove back to London. On my return I went to Glasgow to meet representatives of UCS. I told Tony Hepper that Dr. Taher would like to meet someone in Rome on 2 November who could

21

speak on behalf of UCS. It was agreed that Admiral Scotland would fly to Rome with me for the meeting with Dr. Taher. John Scotland was delighted; he had previously spent two years in Rome as Naval Attaché at the British Embassy and knew the city well.

On 2 November we flew to Rome expecting to meet Dr. Taher that evening. We found a message at the Hotel Excelsior, where we were staying, that he would meet us in his rooms at 12:00 the following day. John and I were pleased to have a free evening in Rome. There was a long discussion about where we should dine. We each had favourite places. John was so enthusiastic about one in particular that it was agreed we should go there. He kept hedging his bet by saying, 'Mind you, it's ten years since I've been there.' It hadn't changed, we had a marvellous meal and because it was a warm night, walked back across half of Rome to the Excelsior.

At noon the next day we went to Dr. Taher's suite. The meeting was very cordial and I think Dr. Taher was gratified to hear a positive justification of the dry dock confirmed by such a knowledgeable man as Admiral Scotland. We all lunched together, after which John and I flew back to London.

We started work on a draft management contract and Ken Douglas met members of the workforce to try to interest them in going out to work in Saudi Arabia. He had prepared a draft service agreement for them to consider which covered a three-year period, with six weeks' home leave after eighteen months on duty. It was pointed out that there would be no tax on the wages earned in Saudi Arabia, and no tax on bringing back to England the money they had saved. He was very persuasive, and by mid-November he told me that he believed he had lined up about half the work force which AGRY would need. Two days later, we were all shocked by the interference of Tony Benn, who bluntly discouraged UCS participation by telling Tony Hepper that it would be better for UCS to sort out its domestic problems on the Clyde rather than enter into an exotic scheme in the Middle East. A disappointed Tony Hepper, Ken Douglas and John Scotland had to forsake the interesting project on which they had worked for a short while. Fortunately, none of this was taken up by the press, so that when the following week I met Sir John Hunter, Chairman of Swan Hunter in Newcastle, he was not aware that we had first approached UCS.

Sir John listened to the outline of the AGRY project and said, of course his company would be able to manage a yard in Saudi Arabia as they had operated a large yard in Malta, and also the former British Naval repair yard in Singapore. He said that Swan Hunter had an experienced team to support their management services, and arranged for me to meet Norman Thompson, his Director of Engineering Services. It was left that

I would report on this discussion to Petromin and I would be in touch after learning their reaction.

I sent Petromin a detailed memorandum about UCS's withdrawal and Swan Hunter's possible interest, together with their background experience in managing overseas ship-repair yards. In those days the postal service in Saudi Arabia was erratic and the only certain way of getting a letter there quickly was to go to BOAC and send it airfreight, after which it was necessary to cable Petromin the airway bill number and someone would then collect it at the airport in Jeddah the following morning.

Two days later Dr. Taher cabled me that Sheikh Yamani would be in Lausanne on 9 December and requested me to bring someone from Swan Hunter to meet with him. Sir John was unable to do so, but he agreed that Norman Thompson could accompany me to Lausanne.

In the mean time there were ten days, during which I had several discussions with Norman Thompson. The intention was to put together some terms of reference which Swan Hunter would require included in their management contract – duration, annual fee, number and trades of personnel provided from Swan Hunter yards, or recruited by them, etc. Of course, it was premature to line up labour and senior staff, as AGRY would take at least two years to build, but Petromin would probably want at least a commitment, or letter of intent, in respect to management services. Petromin would have to pay a retainer until the services could be utilized. We drafted a memorandum ready for Sheikh Yamani to consider.

On 8 December we took an evening flight from London to Geneva and a taxi from Geneva Airport to Lausanne, where we were booked at the Hotel Beaurivage. On the morning of the 9th, Sheikh Yamani saw us briefly. He had various meetings scheduled, but would see us at 16:00. Norman Thompson and I lunched together and he disclosed that he was leaving Swan Hunter to become Managing Director of the Cunard Steamship Company. He was a very able executive, combining an engineering degree with accountancy. (He was later recruited from Cunard to become Chairman of the Hong Kong Subway.) However, he was acting as a Swan Hunter executive when we met with Sheikh Yamani. He confirmed his belief in AGRY and mentioned that he had been in charge of the Singapore yard which Swan Hunter had managed under contract until they had trained the Singaporeans to take over all the functions of the yard. He said he imagined that this would also be the intention of the OAPEC yard, and said he did not foresee any reasons why a dry dock and ship-repairing complex could not be operated successfully in Saudi Arabia, even with no indigenous skilled labour available. As always, Sheikh Yamani was an attentive, intelligent listener, reading the veracity of Norman's words through his steady, penetrating gaze. After Norman had been heard, Sheikh Yamani invited Swan Hunter to send a team to visit Saudi

23

Arabia and investigate the actual conditions so that they could move the dry dock considerations out of the realm of theory. Norman said he would try to arrange for a visit of inspection in January. On the return flight to London, I had an opportunity privately to ask an outgoing Director of Swan Hunter, no longer with a vested interest, whether in his opinion he believed AGRY made sense and could be achieved. He positively stated his opinion 'yes', and I was pleased to have my own views confirmed by an expert.

The Saudi Arabian visit by two management experts from Swan Hunter was arranged for the beginning of February.

On 21 December there was a lunch arranged at home for Dr. Taher, Norman Thompson, Anthony Mackesy and Peter Nash of Swan Hunter, and Jacobo Valdes, a Director of SENER. Marcella was a very good hostess and had an excellent cook. I preferred entertaining at home rather than at restaurants because the atmosphere was very relaxed. The AGRY project was discussed up to the point it had progressed, and a programme of investigation was outlined for the Swan Hunter team which would visit Saudi Arabia in February. Dr. Taher was becoming very well informed and had taken a great interest in AGRY.

There was now nothing more to be done to advance the project until 1970. Marcella and I celebrated the close of a good year at Annabel's and welcomed in the new decade. Annabel's in Berkeley Square, Mayfair was a swinging place in the sixties and was a favourite of both of us. The club belonged to Mark Birley, a man of great taste, who had it superbly decorated. It had the most international and exciting crowd in town, it was good to be seen there and had wonderful music that one could dance to, as well as excellent cuisine.

# 4

# JANUARY – APRIL 1970

My first task in 1970 was to apply again for a Saudi Arabian visa. It was almost impossible to obtain a multiple entry visa. I had even tried through the Ministry of Petroleum and was told multiple entry visas were only given to foreign residents in the Kingdom. So each time I went to the Kingdom I had to repeat the performance of the visa application, but this time they accepted a photostat of my certificate of religion and I did not have to ask Nicolas Rivett-Carnac for a further one. It was always a good idea to allow two weeks lead time between visa application and intended date of departure. I hoped that one day the bureaucracy would speed up, otherwise I could foresee endless complaints from ships' crews who would be confined to the AGRY perimeter fence and not be allowed out of the yard. There was no parallel to AGRY operating in that country. The only large employer of expatriate labour was Aramco. Although personnel without multiple entry visas had to apply each time for a visa, their passports were processed by the Aramco office in San Francisco or New York. Saudi Airlines also employed expatriates, but they were resident in the Kingdom and had multiple entry visas. When the dry dock was built I foresaw that the immigration and drink laws would present difficulties. Imagine ships' crews arriving about 40 at a time every 10 days and being unable to get a drink, even a beer. At this stage I could make no attempt to change the laws of the Kingdom, and waited to see what would evolve. Soon another obstacle appeared, this time connected with religion.

There were a couple of preparatory meetings with Swan Hunter, and I flew to Bilbao to collect the AGRY model incorporating the Abdul Azis Pier, which I wanted to take to Petromin. A convenient carrying case had been made for it, with protective padding, so that it could travel in the baggage compartment of the aircraft.

I flew out to Jeddah on 6 February, Anthony Mackesy and Peter Nash would follow the next day. It was my plan to try and arrange a schedule of meetings, etc., before they arrived. I arrived in Jeddah about 21:00. In February the temperature was very pleasant and not humid. It had been very cold in London and on disembarking from the aircraft the air felt like the Caribbean. What I didn't know was that I was arriving at the beginning of the Hajj, the Holy Pilgrimage to Mecca, at which time hundreds of thousands of Muslims from all over the world arrive at Saudi Arabian ports and airports on both sides of the country and converge on Mecca. The busiest airport during the Hajj is Jeddah, because of its proximity to Mecca. Jeddah Airport could normally handle about one aircraft per hour, but that night in February they were landing every five minutes.

On the tarmac beside the sleek VC10 which had flown me from London, was a mixture of old four-engined and two-engined propeller aircraft, first generation 707s, and quite a few private jets of the devout rich, all having brought believers of the Prophet's exhortation to make the pilgrimage to Mecca, at least once in a lifetime.

The Hajj, and the other important religious event, Ramadan, do not occur on the same date each year, as does Christmas. A lunar calendar is followed in the Muslim world, so that the Hajj and Ramadan edge forward about a fortnight each year. This year in February a comfortable temperature prevailed. I was grateful it had not occurred in August on my previous flight to Jeddah, where the conditions in the immigration and customs hall would have resembled a five-hour wait in a sauna. It was nevertheless an experience to avoid in the future, with tremendous crowding while waiting to hand in passport and clear one's suitcase. Baggage was being collected at random from the various parked aircraft and pulled in the same sort of hand-carts as last August by tired Pakistanis, with a very few cases on each cart so as to reduce the weight being pulled. As it took more than two hours to pass through immigration, with the long line of passengers stretching out on the tarmac, I imagined I would find my case and AGRY model container already in the customs hall, but this did not happen. I am not usually too happy in such situations, as queues and tightly crowded spaces, with a great amount of shoving, toe-treading and sweating humanity usually annoy me, but instead of an agonizing wait, it became an interesting occurrence. There were people of all colours and nationalities, sharing the Muslim faith, good-naturedly enduring part of their pilgrimage with a kind of happy acceptance. I did not see one bad-tempered person, even when they had to submit their various bundles, including cooking and sleeping equipment, to the rather rough probing of the Saudi customs officials. Whole families were making the pilgrimage and seemed to have brought all their possessions with them. Some native costumes were very bright, especially the Sudanese, whose tall, dark-skinned women wore vivid coloured silks and cottons tied around them; there were saris from the Indian Continent, as well as Malaysian, Indonesian and Iranian national dress. I would not wish to repeat the experience, but the eight-hour wait to clear formalities passed, and when I emerged and took a taxi to the Kandarah Palace, I was pleased to have been part of a happening in a part of the world where I had come to try to mount a project needing technical skills, but also requiring a great deal of faith.

I was concerned that there was no way to warn Mackesy and Nash of what to expect that night at Jeddah Airport. The hotel told me a cable would take 24 hours to get to London. There was no telex, and a telephone call would take three to four days as all traffic passed through a radio link.

At 09:00 I telephoned Petromin and spoke to Dr. Taher's secretary who regretted that he was unable to suggest a way to get a message to London in under 24 hours. I telephoned the BOAC office to see if a London-bound crew member would telephone Mr. Mackesy when arriving in London; although there was willingness, it was pointed out that the London flight would arrive subsequently to Mr. Mackesy's departure. Having done all I could to make contact, I breakfasted, slept for a while and then went downstairs to enjoy the sun and the Kandarah pool. The pool was closed the following year by the religious authorities because it had permitted mixed bathing. The austere Wahabi sect of the Muslim faith practised in Saudi Arabia found it offensive to see men and women in swimming costumes in the water at the same time. The strict Wahabi code of behaviour was to have its effect on AGRY also the next year.

I spent the afternoon until dusk at the pool, had a delicious meal of Red Sea snapper in the restaurant and went to bed early, anticipating an angry dawn arousal by Messrs. Mackesy and Nash.

At 6:30 they knocked on my door. I could not even offer a drink to comfort them. I told them there had been no way to contact them, nor had I been able to drive up to the airport steps and whisk them away by car to the Kandarah Palace. Both being well-travelled Englishmen, and reasonable chaps, all was forgiven and we arranged to meet by the pool after they had a sleep. I told them Dr. Taher would meet us at the Petromin office at 21:00. The sun shone as well as it had the previous day and we lunched by the pool. They had prepared a very comprehensive organization chart which they explained. A great deal of thought and paper planning had already been done by Swan Hunter. We spent the whole day talking about AGRY. Mackesy and Nash pointed out all the problems and pluses they foresaw. I was reassured when they showed admiration for SENER's model and told me they thought it depicted a workable dry dock/shiprepair yard.

At 20:30 Petromin's car came to collect us. The office was a few miles out of Jeddah on the Medina road. We were shown into Dr. Taher's office and sat down around a conference table. Mackesy and Nash gave Dr. Taher a copy of their organization chart and explained the functions of each department, numbers of workers required, etc. Dr. Taher asked if they had as yet observed any hindrances to the creation of the dry dock. Mackesy asked whether there was any prospect of lifting the strict visa laws which would hamper engineers, or others, from a shipowner's head office, flying down at short notice to attend a particular ship which was in the yard. Dr. Taher doubted if the immigration laws would change in the foreseeable future. Mackesy and Nash were, of course, too courteous to ask if the prohibition on the sale or consumption of alcohol would be abolished. The meeting was not a long one. I felt, and certainly the perceptive Dr. Taher must have felt, that the two Swan Hunter representatives were not as full of enthusiasm for the project as had been Admiral Scotland. Perhaps the previous night's experience had tired them. When the SENER model was produced, Mackesy and Nash gave a very knowledgeable description of the procedure which would normally be followed when a ship came to the facility for a routine docking and maintenance. At the end of the meeting, Dr. Taher asked how many of the men shown on the organization chart would come from Swan Hunter, and what percentage increase they would have to be paid over their current wages. Mackesy and Nash promised to prepare these figures and have them ready the following day. Dr. Taher said the Minister would like another meeting with us the following morning at 11:00 at the Ministry of Petroleum. We said goodnight and the car drove us back to the hotel.

On the way back the Swan Hunter people expressed doubts about providing AGRY with a homogeneous workforce from their yard in England, as Dr. Taher seemed to want. They felt, at best, they could provide about a dozen of the key people, and would have to recruit the rest, English-speaking workers, from Pakistan or Singapore, which they suggested would reduce labour cost at AGRY as South-east Asian labour would not require overseas pay increments. This seemed a big stumbling-block to me, as I knew Dr. Taher expected that full manning by a prestigious shipyard would enhance the saleability of AGRY.

The meeting with Sheikh Yamani was short and a pure courtesy visit. Presumably he had already been briefed by Dr. Taher. He had no questions of his own. There was another meeting that evening with Dr. Taher. When Mackesy and Nash produced the numbers of people Swan Hunter would provide, and explained the economic advantage of recruiting the balance from Pakistan, which was also a Muslim country, I felt that Dr. Taher was disappointed. After a further short discussion, Dr. Taher thanked them for their visit and said he would have to consider the matter and would advise them through me. Both Mackesy and Nash realized that Dr. Taher gave great importance to the management role being provided by a homogeneous workforce from a well-known shipyard.

On the way back to the hotel Mackesy and Nash confided that Swan Hunter would not be able to provide complete staffing of AGRY, nor would they recommend it as a sensible idea. They said they would leave the next day, and hoped to miss the pilgrims returning from the Hajj. I said they had plenty of time as the exodus would not start for another ten days. I shared their view that the trip could have been avoided if the point about a homogeneous workforce had been raised at our meetings in England.

Dr. Taher's secretary telephoned me the next morning to say that Dr. Taher was in Riyadh at the Petromin head office, but would meet me the following day, Tuesday, at the Jeddah office and would send a car at 9:00. As there was nothing else to do, I spent the day in the sun by the pool. Mackesy and Nash had already left. I thought a great deal about the management and manning of AGRY; in many ways Mackesy and Nash were right. Although they did not mention it, they probably felt that it would be a distinct liability to AGRY to send down a workforce from a British shipyard where efficiency was so severely handicapped by the job demarcation rules insisted upon by the British Unions, almost a different one for each trade. The workforce might adhere to British Union rules, even if no Unions existed or were permitted in Saudi Arabia.

When I met with Dr. Taher, he said there was no point in building AGRY until we had solved the problem of management and manning. His view about using Pakistani workers was that every shipowner would know they were less efficient than Europeans and would be reluctant to send their ship to an inefficient repair yard. He told me to find managers as soon as possible.

I flew to London the next day. When I arrived at home there was a message that Sheikh Yamani wished to meet with me at the Beaurivage in Lausanne the next day (Thursday). I hoped the purpose of the meeting was not to inform me that because of the manning difficulties he and OAPEC had decided to abandon the project. However, I was so convinced AGRY had real validity in the Arabian Gulf that if he had doubts, I felt I could dispel them.

I took the first flight to Geneva, hoping to get to Lausanne in time for a meeting and then return to London the same day. Sheikh Yamani had left a message with Maurice Brunel that he would meet me at 15:00. Maurice and I had lunch together. He told me that he had heard there was progress on the dry dock project.

When we joined Sheikh Yamani he reminded me the dry dock was an OAPEC project, even though Petromin had been charged with exploring it. As such, he said it should be located in the most convenient of the Arabian Gulf OAPEC States, i.e. Saudi Arabia, Kuwait, Bahrain, Qatar, Abu Dhabi or Dubai. He wanted an objective investigation. Saudi Arabia did not want the dry dock located on its shores unless this proved the best solution. Sheikh Yamani said that engineers from SENER should visit Dammam and then go to the other OAPEC countries and prepare a report and recommendation of the optimum location, both from the point of view of building the dry dock and operating it. He also told me that his term as OAPEC's first Secretary General was now expired and he had asked the new Secretary General, Mr. Souheil Sadawi, to telephone me when he came to London in April. He asked me to meet him and bring him up to date on developments with the dry dock project. We parted and I caught my flight back home. I was very saddened by Sheikh Yamani's news. I admired him greatly and a strong personal friendship had developed between us.

On arrival home I telephoned SENER and asked if we could meet the following Monday; they agreed. The next day being Friday, Marcella and I decided to drive down to Spain over the weekend. It would be a good opportunity to try out a new car, a Porsche 911, which I had recently purchased. We spent the night in Nimes at the Hotel de France and proceeded via Barcelona to the Hotel Ritz in Madrid on Sunday night. SENER had requested we meet at their Madrid office instead of Bilbao as previously. Jacobo Valdes was in charge of AGRY for SENER. As far as Marcella and I were concerned, the meeting place was an improvement. The Madrid Ritz was very comfortable with excellent service and restaurant. Bilbao is very like the serious, sombre, industrial cities in the North East of England, but as in England, the people living there were hard-working, reliable and precise in their dealings.

SENER were very pleased with the progress and looked forward to visiting the Arabian Gulf in April to carry out their study of various locations. I asked Jacobo Valdes if he thought we could interest AESA (Astilleros Españoles SA, Spain's largest shipbuilding group, with four yards, one of which could build VLCCs). It might provide a useful combination of skills if SENER could design AGRY to AESA's requirements, and AESA could manage the dry dock/repair yard. Jacobo Valdes said he would try to arrange a meeting with AESA, but felt it would be helpful to have Fernando Azqueta along at the same time as he was one of AESA's biggest shipowner customers. Jacobo Valdes and I met the following day with Fernando Azqueta, who had obligingly come down from Bilbao.

When we met Fernando, Jacobo Valdes and I explained the position *vis-à-vis* UCS and Swan Hunter, and asked whether Fernando believed AESA might be interested in managing AGRY as well as manning it. He replied that he did not know, but he was of the impression that there was a surplus of labour at the shipyards due to more automation having been introduced and the closing of one of the very old shipyards in the group. He said he would arrange an appointment with the Chairman and Managing Director of the group. He telephoned AESA and learned both were away at various meetings, but he was able to fix a meeting with the two at the head office in Madrid for 5 March. It meant waiting a further two weeks to learn if AESA was interested. We spent the next day planning a schedule of visits by Jacobo Valdes' team to the Gulf, starting with Dammam, then Kuwait, Bahrain, Qatar, Abu Dhabi and Dubai.

They had to obtain visas but there was adequate time before the April visit. We hoped they might be joined by someone from AESA, which would make it a really useful trip. The following day Marcella and I drove back to London. I was back home for the weekend after two weeks of absence in Saudi Arabia, Switzerland, France and Spain. I had a lot of paper work to consume.

The time in between travel was spent in London working on AGRY – letters, progress reports to Petromin, studies and cash flow projections, as I was still trying to find a way to establish financial viability for the yard. There were two of us to handle all the paper work, Sylvia Cape, in the North of England, and myself. While in London I gave lunches almost every day at home for such diverse groups as representatives of the insurance world, oil company marine departments, classification societies, salvage society, shipowners, Lloyd's List and other press. A great deal of information was being collected and collated. AGRY was beginning to appear in the press, and comment from such serious sources as Richard Johns in the *Financial Times*, was adding to the credibility of the project and obviated a lot of explaining at first meetings as people had read about it.

On 5 March I flew back to Madrid and, accompanied by Fernando Azqueta and Jacobo Valdes, met with Mr. Claudio Abado, the Chairman of AESA. Fernando made a preliminary summary in Spanish, and then the conversation switched back to English, in which I was relieved to see Mr. Abado was fluent. I more or less repeated what had been said, namely that the Arabian Gulf Repair Yard had come to a standstill as Petromin would not consider its building until a suitable manager had been found, and that Dr. Taher was convinced that the manager should provide its own workforce.

Mr. Abado said he could not even indicate an interest at this point on behalf of AESA, but he proposed that we meet again in ten days, at which time he would merely say no, or if AESA believed that further investigation was merited, at the next meeting he would introduce me to the AESA representative who would continue the dry dock project examination. We agreed the next meeting should take place in Madrid on 16 March.

At the 16 March meeting, Mr. Abado introduced Fernando del Molino, Manager of the Cadiz VLCC AESA yard, and Luis Asophros, its Repair Manager. Also present was Jacobo Valdes of SENER. The meeting commenced with a general presentation of AGRY and what its OAPEC principals hoped it would achieve. I was pleased to learn that the Spanish press had picked up the AGRY story, as well as the shipping journals. Of course, SENER's involvement as the leading Spanish marine engineering group

31

was news. Del Molino said AESA was interested, but could only envisage rendering a partial service. This would be for operating the dry dock and providing all work on the hull and piping of the ship, but they must exclude machinery, especially any work on the sophisticated turbines and gears of the VLCC. He said that AESA built Sulzer diesel engines under licence for their smaller ships and imported turbines from Japan, or sometimes America, which were installed, tested, and even later, repaired by their manufacturers. He did not see a problem in providing a homogeneous Spanish workforce from AESA, but restricted to hull work. We seemed at least half-way there. Del Molino suggested that I meet with a Japanese turbine manufacturer rather than an American one, which of course would be more expensive, particularly when it meant providing an on site staff and workforce at AGRY. He pointed out a further advantage in approaching Japan, saying that more than 70 per cent of all VLCCs built would probably have Japanese propulsion machinery. He said that Japan was preparing to build 90 VLCCs per year in six of their biggest shipyards. There were five main Japanese manufacturers of turbines for VLCCs. AESA used both Kawasaki and Mitsubishi. When asked if AESA would consider a joint venture with a Japanese company which would be responsible for machinery repairs, Del Molino said not on a 50/50 basis but, say, 60/40, with AESA having 60 per cent as they would be providing the majority of labour, whilst Japan would send out only some highly skilled technicians who would be assisted by the AESA labour, just as took place in Spain when installing turbines.

The conversation then became largely hypothetical, but it was agreed that Del Molino would join Jacobo Valdes in April to visit Saudi Arabia.

A beginning had been made again, and I flew back to London. What remained for the moment an unsolved situation was which machinery manufacturer would join in the venture to provide turbine expertise. It seemed pointless to approach the Japanese on a conditional basis, which must be the case until AESA had given their agreement to participate in the management. This might happen after their visit to the Arabian Gulf in April.

In the mean time, more and more press comment began to appear, together with speculation about the first pan-Arabic industrial project of the two-year-old OAPEC. A favourable view of a repair yard in the Arabian Gulf was beginning to emerge following an explosion on a Norwegian VLCC which had to be towed around the coast of Africa back to Lisbon at a very considerable cost.

At the beginning of April I returned to Madrid for a further meeting with AESA and SENER. They had decided to leave for Saudi Arabia on 20 April. Del Molino and Jacobo Valdes would fly to Dharhan on the

Gulf coast, and from there visit the nearby Dammam pier. On the first visit they would concentrate on that area and get the feel of the place, both from construction and operational points of view.

# 5

# APRIL – OCTOBER 1970

The following week I met Mr. Souheil Sadawi, the new Secretary General of OAPEC, at his suite in the London Hilton. His professional training had been as a lawyer, and he had little exposure to oil or shipping. When he asked why OPEC should want to build a dry dock, I really felt that we were starting at the beginning. An hour later I departed. For the first time I had met a real obstacle, but I tried to console myself with the argument that Mr. Sadawi would not be making all the decisions. One useful effect the meeting had was that from now on I realized I would not be dealing with a sympathetic audience, and that my facts and the logic of AGRY must be unassailable. It was always easier to prove what was wrong with a new idea than what was right about it. Fortunately, I had come to learn from the inside more than anyone about what was wrong with the project and was fluent at counteracting criticism of AGRY. Nevertheless, a number of meetings were arranged to test market opinion among oil company and independent shipowners, classification societies, and Lloyd's underwriters. The sampling was as before. Shipowners all agreed it would be helpful to their operations to have AGRY, and said it would be used subject to quality, cost and repair time being competitive. The classification societies and underwriters favoured it, but of course no revenue for AGRY would come from them. As yet I had not found a single insurmountable snag thrown up by potential users. All of these discussions were gradually convincing more and more people that AGRY would be built, particularly with the financial muscle of Saudi Arabia, and OAPEC apparently sponsoring it.

On 26 April Jacobo Valdes, Del Molino and I met at Beirut Airport and joined the same flight for Dharhan. Dharhan had a much more modern airport – at least the passenger buildings – than Jeddah. We quickly cleared customs and immigration, in almost half the time of Jeddah. We went to the Airport Hotel. This was a disappointment compared to Jeddah. The hotel was a collection of Nissan huts with deteriorated amenities. I would have preferred to arrive a week earlier, and try to clean and brighten up the Airport Hotel to improve the impression it made on the Spanish visitors. At dinner that evening, Del Molino said he had to chase the cucarachas out of the shower before he could use it. None of the window air conditioners worked, which didn't matter so much in April.

My dual role of convincing Arab principals of the merit of AGRY required some selling. Also, selling was required to convince its future managers that the Arabian Gulf was an ideal location in which to operate AGRY.

The next morning Mr. Al Saban, a representative from Petmark, the Petromin marketing company, collected us and we drove to Dammam pier and met the Pakistani port captain. We were shown all over the facility, which looked very efficient. The port captain was not at all enthusiastic about AGRY being sited adjacent to the pier because, as he disclosed, they were planning an extension to the port complex by building a parallel pier exactly where the SENER drawing showed AGRY would be situated. We spent the morning at Dammam port and after lunch had a meeting with Dr. Taher. He knew of the problem connected with the Dammam location and said he had arranged for a small aircraft to fly us at low altitude up and down the coast to see whether any area recommended itself to us visually.

The next morning we went to the airport and Capt. Rickett met us. He and I instantly recognized each other as we had both been flying for Air Transport Command during the Second World War. Neither of us had apparently changed unrecognizably in the intervening quarter-century. Rickett was now a pilot for TWA which were operators of Saudia, the Saudi Arabian National Airline. He led us to a DC3 which was used for internal flights and pilot training. We took off and spent about three hours cruising 'low and slow' above the coast. For most of the time Rickett let me do the flying. Twenty-three years had passed since I last flew a DC3, but flying is like riding a bicycle, and in both cases, when you return to it after along absence you tend to over-control until you get your balance. I thoroughly enjoyed it, but was relieved he did not invite me to make the landing.

There was no reasonable location that any one of us spotted. There was very shallow water extending for several miles from the coast, and of course no infrastructure in the way of roads, which meant a large amount of dredging to create a channel to deep water and the building of roads, etc., all of which would add enormously to the cost of AGRY.

We met Dr. Taher again, who accepted the difficulties of siting AGRY in Saudi Arabia and suggested AESA, SENER and I go to Kuwait to investigate possibilities there. We flew to Kuwait from Dharhan, Petromin having arranged our visas. These formalities are carried out much more quickly locally then in London at the Consulates of Arab Countries. Perhaps they had been instructed to slow down the rush of business hopefuls who were making their way to the Arabian Peninsula in a steady stream.

My Spanish colleagues were impressed with the Kuwait Sheraton, which shone like an oasis after the Dharhan Airport Hotel. We were again frustrated in our site investigation because the same shallow water extended along the coastline up to the head of the Gulf. In some ways, not finding the right location in Kuwait was not a disappointment as there was an even greater paucity of indigenous labour than in Saudi Arabia. Also, Kuwait was too far up the Gulf for the majority of VLCCs which would be loading 300–500 miles to the south at Ras Tanura, meaning a deviation of at least one day's steaming to reach AGRY if it were sited there.

We agreed to investigate Bahrain, Qatar, Abu Dhabi and Dubai on a future visit as both Del Molino and Valdes had to return to Spain. We all flew to Beirut late that same afternoon and made connections with onward flights to Madrid and London. We regretted not having the time to spend a couple of days in Beirut which was then enjoying its last fling.

On the flight to London I had five hours to realize that, well into the second year of AGRY pursuit, we had made very little progress as to coming to terms with a manager, or even selecting a site. At the moment we did not even know in which Gulf State the dry dock/repair yard would be located.

In the week following my return to London I was not able to make any progress towards the AGRY realization, and at the end of the week I received a cable from Dr. Taher requesting me to make a full feasibility study, based on all data obtained to date, for presentation to the next OAPEC Ministerial Conference. He said that Maurice Brunel would be coming to London on 17 May and that a draft of the study should be ready to discuss with him. That gave me ten days in which to put it together and, I hoped, be able to include something new of a positive nature.

The new material I was able to assemble consisted of a definitive list from the two main classification societies of all dry docks, whether for building or repair, of VLCCs that existed or were planned world-wide. I also obtained a list of all VLCCs in existence, or on order, giving name of owner, exact vessel size, and building yard. These two lists, when used together, and assuming an average docking cycle of 18 months, convincingly showed that there were too few dry docks for the number of VLCCs, even assuming that building docks would be used 50 per cent of the time for repair purposes. The shortfall was 12 dry docks. Certainly there was a need for AGRY and this was the first time I had been able statistically to show this.

Maurice Brunel met me in London and went over the draft study in careful scrutiny. Maurice made some helpful suggestions as to format, but the main changes were to reduce the text and to include all supporting documentation in the appendix, with a further section for plans and drawings. Maurice said that the OAPEC Ministerial Conference would take place in Algiers on Saturday, 27 June, and that I should attend and be prepared to answer questions about the dry dock. (It was sometimes called that and sometimes AGRY – the Arab Nationals tended to call it the dry dock as AGRY was very similar to an Arabic word for something unpleasant! The name would have to be changed if there was a decision to build it.)

Maurice told me that the secretariat of OAPEC liked to have all documentation to be considered at least 30 days prior to the meeting, and would require 25 copies for the Ministers and their staff. Usually, documents presented in languages other than Arabic were translated, or if this was not possible, such as in the case of the dry dock, a summary of the main text was made in Arabic. There was at that time no Arabic word for 'dry dock'.

On 25 May I flew to Madrid to meet with SENER and AESA to get their clearance on the sections of the report for which they had supplied the input. Neither wanted any changes and I flew back to London the same day in order to deliver the study to the printers in time to despatch it by airfreight to Kuwait on Friday, 29 May. Friday is a holiday in the Arab world, equivalent to our Sunday. The report arrived in Kuwait on Saturday, 30 May at the beginning of the Arab working week.

There was not much which I could do or change before the meeting in Algiers, so Marcella and I decided to drive to Greece for a holiday with sun and sea. Just before leaving I received a telephone call from SENER asking urgently for a meeting in Bilbao on 2 June. Since their visit to Saudi Arabia they had been very active and had prepared locational drawings for Bahrain, Qatar, Abu Dhabi and Dubai. They had sent their engineers to the four countries. Valdes said that up to his latest information he had always considered the expansion of Dammam port a plus, because it would be easier to construct something supported by an infrastructure and where dredging was already envisaged, but now he felt differently and was able to recommend two better locations – Bahrain and Dubai. Qatar and Abu Dhabi had to be ruled out for a number of technical reasons. This news was interesting, but it was too late to incorporate in the study, now in the hands of the OAPEC secretariat. I asked him to prepare a small study on SENER's findings in Bahrain and Dubai, and I would take 25 copies with me to Algiers. If Sheikh Yamani or Dr. Taher wished them included, they could appear as an addendum.

On my return from Bilbao, Marcella and I started our holiday by car. We drove to Athens, via Brussels, Salzburg and Belgrade. We stayed at a hotel with bungalows outside Athens by the name of Lagonissi. It was new and not quite broken in, with good accommodation and poor food, which we didn't mind as we always preferred to eat in tavernas by the port rather than in hotel dining-rooms. The bungalow faced the sea, with only a few steps down to the water. We had arrived with mosquito nets, so we slept well and spent slightly more than two weeks, with almost continuous good weather. Every now and then, one of the staff from the hotel came running down to the waterside with a long white telex strip over his shoulder. These were from SENER, sending me drafts of sections of their report to agree and possibly improve on the English from time to time. We were all concerned with presentation. I had learned over the past two years that facts were important, but wording was also to be watched lest it offend. Arabian officials were very sensitive to statements which were written in too positive a manner, such as 'this will certainly happen'. They felt that only Allah was allowed to be sure of anything. Of course, such worldly Western exposed stars as Sheikh Yamani, and pragmatic Dr. Taher, were used to Occidental over-sell and were able to discount it. Less sophisticated members of OAPEC might react differently.

Because of the many sections of SENER's study, I worked about an hour each evening composing long telexes in reply. That was good, as it made sure I would not forget AGRY. Marcella knew Greece better than I, so we drove to various monuments, and particularly loved the Poseidon ruin left standing on Cape Sounion. We had a number of Greek ship-owner friends who were not yet on holiday. They were as curious about AGRY as I was to learn their reactions. The general consensus was that they would not be among the first to put their VLCCs into AGRY, but afterwards they would. They all accepted that it would be a useful facility that should certainly be used extensively.

It became time to return home. We drove from Brindisi to Florence, where we spent the night with Marcella's sister. As I had to be away almost as soon as I returned to London, Marcella remained in Florence and I drove on to London.

Back in London on 24 June, I had a meeting with Jack Hartshorn, whose interest continued in AGRY's development. I took an afternoon flight to Madrid and had a working dinner with SENER. They had done a very professional job on their report and gave me 25 copies to take to Algiers.

The following morning from Madrid I flew to Paris and caught a flight to Algiers. OAPEC had booked me into the Hotel St. George, where the Conference delegates were staying. On alighting from the taxi at the hotel, the first person I saw was Maurice Brunel. He told me that both Sheikh Yamani and Dr. Taher would be attending the meeting. We had dinner in the hotel and then called on Sheikh Yamani in case he wanted any information for the following day's meeting. As always he was cordial and asked if I still thought the dry dock was a good idea. When I replied in the affirmative, he said he was pleased because he believed it was an excellent first pan-Arabic industrial venture wherein there was no conflict of interest which might be the case with an oil-related venture. This was good news and I looked forward to the next day's meeting.

The St. George was a delightful old hotel, situated in a garden and overlooking the town and port of Algiers. Maurice Brunel and I had breakfast outdoors under a trellis which ran along the side of the hotel and from which grew a fragrant yellow vine, probably jasmine.

At about 9:00 the Ministers entered the conference room in the hotel, the former ballroom. Maurice and I sat on a sofa in the lobby and waited to be called to answer questions about AGRY, or the dry dock as it was called there. The meeting broke for lunch without either of us being summoned.

Dr. Taher came out and told us that OAPEC had approved proceeding with further studies of the dry dock to try and bring the project to fruition. He said he would like to speak to SENER again, and asked me to telephone them to send someone to Paris, where he would like to meet at the George V Hotel the following day. He asked Maurice and me to fly to Paris with him that afternoon.

It was unable to reach Jacobo Valdes by telephone from Algiers, but I got through to Madrid by telex and he confirmed that he would come to Paris. Dr. Taher, Maurice and I had a relaxed dinner in Paris that evening. Dr. Taher was in a very candid mood, and disclosed that OAPEC were keen to proceed with the dry dock. I was cautionary and reminded him that he had said there was no point in building the dry dock without managers, and that they were still lacking. 'You'll find them,' he said. I asked whether Saudi Arabia would be disappointed if the dry dock was built in another OAPEC country. Dr. Taher said, 'Not really, our traditions hamper establishing another large expatriate community in the Kingdom; we have just digested Aramco after more than 30 years.' However, he still wished us to explore possibilities in Dammam.

Then Dr. Taher asked me to buy, for his account, a motor boat, and to find out how it could be shipped to Jeddah. He said he had a weekend (Thursday and Friday) house on what was called the Creek, north of Jeddah, on an inlet from the Red Sea. He wanted something fast enough for his sons to water-ski, but also something comfortable in which he could go fishing.

Dr. Taher, Maurice and I met Jacobo Valdes on the next day. Valdes explained in detail the site investigations SENER had made, and mentioned that his report found only Bahrain and Dubai suitable, and of the two he favoured Bahrain because of its larger indigenous population and more evolved life-style. Dr. Taher was non-committal and asked him not to drop the consideration of Dammam as a possible site, pointing out that the dry dock might just complement the port expansion. This was also Valdes' idea. The meetings over, Dr. Taher and Maurice flew back to

Jeddah, Valdes to Madrid, and I to London, where it seemed I hadn't been for a very long time. The OAPEC meeting had been positive, but we still had no managers, and I began to explore in my mind which shipyard to approach if AESA said no.

I went in search of a boat for Dr. Taher. After visiting three showrooms, I finally selected what seemed the most suitable craft. It was about 28 foot overall, with a cabin in which an air-conditioner would be installed. It was powered by two large Mercury outboards capable of a speed of about 30 mph. There was a small auxiliary outboard for manœuvring it in port without starting the big engines. It could also be pushed along at slow speed without much wake if leisurely fishing were needed. I paid for it and began to wonder how to ship it down to Jeddah at the least cost. Norman Thompson was by now Managing Director of Cunard, and Cunard ran a cargo liner service between the UK and Jeddah. Norman offered to have the boat shipped to Jeddah as deck cargo if I could arrange for it to be transported to Southampton.

By the end of the week there was a cable from Dr. Taher asking me to meet him in Cairo on 9 July. I flew down and booked into the Nile Hilton, to find that Dr. Taher was across on the other bank of the Nile at the newer Sheraton. We had dinner together on the terrace of his suite on the top floor of the Sheraton, which had a spectacular view of the Nile and a large part of Cairo, which looked better at night than by day. My room at the Hilton faced the opposite direction and I had a view of the pyramids, which appeared pink in the sunset. I had first visited Cairo immediately after the war when I was a pilot for KLM. It had become much bigger, noisier and dirtier since Farouk had been replaced by President Nasser.

Dr. Taher asked if I was prepared to renew my consultancy agreement with Petromin, and offered a substantial increase in fee, which I accepted. I did not believe then, or at any time, that my position as dry dock leader for Petromin was a secure one. Arabs are very changeable; one moment a person is in favour, the next he is discarded. However, I was committed to the realization of AGRY and there was no alternative to Arab sponsors. Each change in prospective managers, or any other component, presented a great risk to the project as it might incur OAPEC irritation, boredom with the length of time it took, or even a decision to change consultant to someone who might appear to them more efficient.

Dr. Taher looked forward to receiving his boat and gave me a cheque for its cost. I stayed another day in Cairo at Dr. Taher's request as he wanted me to speak about the dry dock to a representative of Kuwait, Mr. Adel Al-Hamad. The purpose was to explain the technical requirements of the site, such as water depth, etc. Clearly it was desirable not to offend Kuwait if the dry dock had to be located elsewhere.

On Sunday, 12 July I returned to London. I had caught an ear infection

41

from swimming in the Nile Hilton pool and wanted it treated. The summer season had begun, and as far as Spain was concerned there would be no progress from either AESA or SENER until the beginning of September, when the various executives returned from holiday. I tried to force the pace, especially with AESA, as I felt they would take a long time to make up their minds about the management contract. SENER was quite different as it consisted of a very energetic, aggressive team of bright young engineers hoping to get started.

At the end of July I flew down to Bilbao to see Fernando Azqueta to try to obtain his objective opinion as to whether AESA would participate in the management contract. Fernando gave a number of well-considered reasons why they would, and equally well-considered reasons why they would not be interested. He felt that if they could obtain the conditions they wanted, it was probable that they were ready to assume the majority management role. I believed it might be possible to make them reach a decision more quickly if I could find a Japanese manufacturer which would join with them. I was keen to line up a first-class introduction to either Kawasaki or Mitsubishi, both excellent builders of turbines – alas, this had to wait until executives returned to work. Eventually an introduction appeared from a most unexpected source, and none could have been better.

During the first two weeks of August, I gave some lunches to the shipping press and to the *Financial Times*. It seemed helpful to disclose some solid justification on behalf of AGRY, and to 'come clean' about the present position without definite managers, and the plan to approach a Japanese machinery manufacturer. This produced some helpful coverage and as is well known, things that are written about in the press begin to develop an acceptance and credibility.

In the middle of August, Marcella and I got in the car and headed for Arras and the Hotel de l'Universe, and from there to Milan, over the Simplon Pass, and down to Grosseto on the coast, where we stayed until the beginning of September. We both enjoyed long car trips in the 911, which challenged distances like no other breed of car we have ever owned. The weather was indifferent, as it frequently can be at the end of August and early in September, but the beach was long and we could walk at the water's-edge for an hour in either direction, absorbing a lot of iodine.

On 14 September I flew to Kuwait to attend another OAPEC Conference and, if needed, to answer questions on AGRY (down there it was still 'the dry dock'). Mr. Serrano of SENER joined me as he wished to obtain official approval to re-visit sites in Bahrain and Dubai. I had a much more friendly talk with Mr. Souheil Sadawi, who now realized that OAPEC was considering a dry dock and that I wasn't trying to promote some kind of confidence trick. He wrote an official letter on OAPEC letterhead to enable Mr. Serrano to receive Government help when he visited Bahrain and Dubai.

After the OAPEC meeting, which again approved continuing with the dry dock investigations, Mr. Serrano and I flew to Bahrain. I was only on the ground for a couple of hours while waiting to take a flight to Dharhan, a very short trip away (20 minutes). It felt like being in a British colony. It was at that time a British protectorate and there were lots of British uniforms about. An English soldier frisked me (this was before metal detectors which automatically perform the frisking), before boarding the aircraft. Immigration formalities had been carried out by the British also. I spent the night in that haven, the Airport Hotel in Dharhan, which seemed to have improved. A coat of paint made a big difference, and the air-conditioner in my room worked – in fact, it was a new machine; it was really a relief on that hot, humid, airless night.

I met Dr. Taher on the morning of 19 September (Saturday) and told him I would like to go to Japan to discuss the dry dock with a manufacturer of turbines. He told me that those decisions were mine to make as long as I was in charge of the dry dock investigation. We flew together to Riyadh, Petromin's head office being situated in the capital of Saudi Arabia. I stayed on the aircraft and flew to Jeddah to catch a VC10 to London. We had all boarded, but the steps were still drawn up to the first-class compartment at the front of the aircraft. I was looking out of the window and saw what appeared to be an honour guard of 12 soldiers, six on each side of the steps. Two black Cadillac limousines with the Saudi Arabian coat of arms (featuring sword, palm tree and verse from the Koran in Arabic calligraphy) drove up. Two Japanese men alighted from each car, accompanied by a Saudi Arabian dignitary. The guard snapped to attention and the four Japanese shook hands with their Saudi Arabian hosts, walked up the steps two by two, and occupied two rows of seats on the opposite side of the aisle from me, within hearing distance, but talking in Japanese which I didn't speak. Once we were airborne, I sent a note to the Captain asking if he would kindly inform me who the senior Japanese was. He replied that it was Mr. Kishi, the Minister of Industry.

After drinks had been served, and I noted the Japanese seemed to be drinking appreciatively, not having had an alcoholic drink during their visit to Saudi Arabia, I respectfully introduced myself to Mr. Kishi and explained I was looking for a Japanese manufacturer of ship turbines to join in a venture that was being sponsored by Saudi Arabia and OAPEC. He was very polite, excused himself because of his poor English, and introduced me to his aide, Mr. Michio Kawabe. Mr. Kawabe came to sit in the empty seat beside me and I explained about AGRY. He spoke perfect Californian English – he had a Masters degree in business administration from Stanford. He said such a project might be interesting for

Japan. He told me that he and Minister Kishi were staying at Claridges in London and asked me to call upon him Monday afternoon at 16:00 when he would be able to introduce me to the head of the London office of one of Japan's 'great' trading companies. He explained that one never approached major industries directly, but always through a trading company, of which there were four 'great' ones in Japan – Mitsubishi, Marubeni, C. Itoh and Mitsui. He said each was as good as the other, but were connected with different industries in which they were often large shareholders. He asked which turbine company I preferred. I told him Kawasaki had the greatest reputation world-wide. He said, 'Ahhh sooo', which I thought was very Japanese, and then went on to tell me that C. Itoh represented Kawasaki, and that Mr. Iseki of C. Itoh would be with him at Claridges on Monday. In this fortuitous manner I obtained the best possible introduction to Kawasaki.

On 22 September I went to the appointment with Mr. Kawabe at Claridges and he introduced me to Mr. K. Iseki, who was General Manager of the London office of C. Itoh. I outlined the AGRY project and told him of our search for managers, mentioning AESA who wanted a partner responsible for turbines and other sophisticated machinery. I pointed out that as AESA worked in Spain with Kawasaki, which provided the turbines for the VLCCs AESA built, it seemed appropriate that AESA and Kawasaki might collaborate also in the Arabian Gulf. Mr. Iseki said he would relay all this to Kawasaki by telex. He remarked that of course anything involving co-operation with Saudi Arabia and other Arab oil producers was always interesting to Japan. He recommended that if Kawasaki indicated an interest, I should fly to Tokyo for a meeting.

Things moved fast. He telephoned me two days later and invited me to his office. He received me accompanied by an assistant. I was to learn that it was difficult to have a one-to-one meeting with Japanese. They seemed to like witnesses, although they explained it as training of junior staff. Mr. Iseki told me that Kawasaki would like to meet with me in Tokyo to discuss the matter. I would be busy with AESA in Spain, but I would be able to go at the beginning of October. We formally took leave of each other and he sent me home in a company car.

I made an appointment with AESA for the following week. In Madrid there was a long discussion with Mr. Del Molino, Mr. Arias, an AESA Director, and Jacobo Valdes of SENER. AESA felt I was pushing things too fast, but Jacobo Valdes was delighted that AESA was being pressured, because if Kawasaki were willing, then AESA would have to declare themselves one way or the other. AESA said that if Kawasaki were interested, they would join me in a visit to Tokyo to discuss the matter, followed by a joint AESA/Kawasaki visit to the Arabian Gulf.

On Saturday, 10 October I flew to Tokyo over Moscow. Sitting in the seat next to mine was a very stylish, dignified Japanese, in his sixties. All during the long flight we exchanged no word. When drinks were served he bowed slightly; I raised my glass to him. Japanese Air Lines (JAL) had provided comfortable in-flight slippers which I substituted for my shoes. As we approached Tokyo, I reached for my shoes but could not put them on as my feet had swelled during the long flight. After observing my struggles for several minutes, my Japanese neighbour reached into his overnight bag and produced an elegant ivory shoehorn which he offered me. I thanked him, and applied it to my shoe. To my horror I broke it. After apologizing shamefacedly, I asked him for his card so that I might send him a replacement. His name was Mr. Sotto and he was President of the Japanese Chamber of Shipping. After flying 13 hours in silence, we talked animatedly for the last 15 minutes until landing. (I sent him a shoehorn from London which he must have considered an honourable replacement as we met cordially on several subsequent occasions in Japan.)

I was very jet-lagged on arrival, but went out for a short walk on what was a mild autumn afternoon. On returning to the Imperial Hotel, I explored the extensive shopping arcade, bought Marcella a silk kimono, and looked at all the tiny bugging devices and other electronic and photographic displays. When I got back to my room there was a message from C. Itoh that I would be collected on Monday morning at 9:00 and taken to the offices of Kawasaki. Before departing from London, I had not told C. Itoh at which hotel I was staying, or which flight I was taking, only that I would telephone the C. Itoh office on Monday morning to learn what programme had been arranged. I did not want to put anyone to the nuisance of meeting me at the airport on Sunday morning, so I took a taxi to the Imperial Hotel. I did not mention the hotel for the same reason, to spare some junior his Sunday without having to offer me hospitality. It was the last time I was able to arrive when on a business trip without being met at the airport, or finding a basket of fruit or flowers in my hotel room. An office at Tokyo Airport had the passenger manifest of all incoming, as well as departing, flights. Companies expecting a visitor need only telephone and give the name of the visitor to learn the arrival time; also, every hotel informs a central office of the names and home country of its guests booked on each day. Thus, companies easily find out in which hotel their visitor is staying. To arrive in Tokyo anonymously for a business meeting is not easy to achieve. I found out on one occasion that the restaurant I had dined in was known. This was easy to establish if one went by taxi from the hotel. Tokyo taxi drivers have problems understanding names of places given in English, so the practice is to ask the doorman for a taxi and tell him your destination, which he writes on a piece of paper and gives to the cab driver – so the hotel knows where one has gone, at least the first stop.

I always enjoyed my visits to Japan. In spite of it being very crowded,

Tokyo and its inhabitants are agreeable. I have never boarded a subway in the rush hour, but have been told that although travellers are packed in very tight, a sort of remoteness descends on the passengers, who withdraw to their own thoughts and never become aggressive being pushed or trodden upon because they are absent until the train stops at their destination. I noticed above all that Tokyo has been much influenced in matters such as fast food, entertainment and speech, by their major trading partner, the USA.

# 6

# OCTOBER – NOVEMBER 1970

Mr. Masuda of C. Itoh telephoned at 18:00 to welcome me and ask if there was anything I needed. He re-confirmed that he would be calling for me at 9:00 in the morning, and asked me to be near the front door of the hotel as parking was only allowed for a very short time.

International Japanese hotels in Tokyo are very well equipped with all the amenities. Additional to the shopping arcades, there are Japanese, Chinese, French, Italian, steak, sea-food and snack restaurants. There are all business services – secretarial, telex, fax, photocopying, etc. There is a swimming pool, indoor tennis, sauna and massage service available to guests. In the central hall, all year round, there is a tree in blossom. It lasts a week and then an expert team come in, take it out, and another is erected. All come from the hotel's own greenhouses. Room service arrives speedily, and is impeccably served. The Tokyo air was polluted, and a new smell added to the carbon dioxide, that of burnt propane. The taxis, and many private cars, were operating on propane (LP-gas) instead of petrol; the exhaust is supposed to be less toxic and certainly smelled better.

The purity of Japanese art is manifest in their beautiful calligraphy, extending to the making of a rose from a carrot by a few quick and deft strokes of a knife.

On Monday morning the C. Itoh car arrived punctually and we were driven through dense traffic to the World Trade Centre skyscraper, where Kawasaki have their offices. The lift ascended to the 25th floor and we stepped out into a reception area. We gave our names and seconds later Mr. Toshio Kawakami, Overseas Sales Manager, came out to greet us. He took us in to meet Dr. Yoshida, the Managing Director, who looked very much like an idealized Samurai. Both spoke excellent, easy flowing, English.

They asked me to describe the dry dock project, and how I considered Kawasaki might help. I concentrated on the present position and did not go into any of the history, or refer to any shipyard other than AESA. Refreshments were served – coffee, fruit drinks, Coca-Cola, and small sandwiches. Afterwards, Dr. Yoshida said we would go into the Boardroom where we would meet Mr. Hasegawa, the Vice-President of the Shipbuilding and Turbine Division, together with some technical people. The Boardroom was huge, with an extremely long table in the centre which must have been capable of seating 60.

Mr. Hasegawa was a very gruff man, with protruding teeth and almost invisible eyes. He was very strongly built. He crunched my fingers when we shook hands, pointed to the other side of the table and said, 'You sit there'. Across from me sat Mr. Hasegawa, with Dr. Yoshida on his right, and Mr. Kawakami on his left. Ranged symmetrically six on the right of Mr. Kawakami and six on the left of Dr. Yoshida, were engineers, and maybe even petroleum experts, naval architects, or crude oil traders. My acquaintance from C. Itoh had disappeared, so I was sure that C. Itoh would be sent a comprehensive transcript of all the proceedings.

Mr. Hasegawa wanted to hear the whole story from the beginning. He said he understood AESA's position and agreed that Kawasaki assistance on turbines would be beneficial to AGRY. It would make tedious reading to relate the entire three-hour meeting, but it can be said that the Japanese were very thorough and exhaustive in their questioning, in which every aspect of AGRY was touched upon, some of which was new to me and hasty improvising was required. At 13:30 Mr. Hasegawa announced, 'We lunch', and led the way, followed by Dr. Yoshida, Mr. Kawakami and myself. In a small private lift we went up to the top floor of the building where there were two excellent restaurants, one French and one Chinese, together with a panoramic view of Tokyo, and as it was a clear day, also of Mount Fuji, with its cap of snow. Luncheon conversation did not touch on AGRY, but instead began by comparing oil production levels of Saudi Arabia and Iran, and the observation that Japan was largely dependent on oil imports from the Middle East. There was more than a casual dropping of hints, and a steering towards oil, as if to suggest that co-operation of Kawasaki might be made easier if, somehow, oil could become a part of the consideration. After lunch we shook hands and Mr. Kawakami said he would take me down to the car which would take me back to the hotel. He was very entertaining, and cracked a few jokes about the Japanese way of doing business. He could pronounce perfectly the word 'inscrutable' without the usual Japanese difficulty with 'r'. I left the building with not the slightest clue as to whether Kawasaki would be interested in joining in the management role of AGRY.

I got back to the hotel, left my briefcase in my room, and wandered about Tokyo. A good friend of mine was a model railway buff with a large collection. He had asked me to look for a certain American steam locomotive which was made by a well-known Japanese model manufacturer. I found the shop he had described and have never seen such beautiful models of trains, 'planes and cars. Each one was more than a toy, resembling the type of precision in the showcases of the Science Museum in London. They had the particular engine my friend wanted and I purchased it. They packed it well in an expanded polythene case which was made to fit it. As it was rather heavy to carry around, I walked back to the hotel to leave it in my room, planning to go out again. However, I found a message from Mr. Ogawa of C. Itoh saying that they would like me to dine with them that night and would be calling for me at 18:30, which left little time to shower and change clothes.

They took me to Maxims, apparently a bona fide branch of the Paris Maxims. My preference would have been for oriental food, having had a heavy French lunch with Kawasaki. In any case, I was much more interested in hearing from C. Itoh about the Kawasaki meeting than in food. There were two other executives of C. Itoh, Mr. Kai, quite senior, and Mr. Kakizawa. They were very hospitable, and insisted that we start with caviar, followed by a small fish course and Châteaubriand. Good business for Maxims, but bad business for my digestive system, so we eliminated the fish course and substituted entrecôte for the Châteaubriand, and also reduced the number of wines ordered. I was unable to determine whether it was a case of the prisoner being offered a good meal prior to execution, or whether they were wooing a prospective big business deal. As always in Japanese discussion, there was an amount of good humoured giggling, especially when I tried to talk about Kawasaki, and after a burst of laughter was told 'in office tomorrow'. They really only wanted to talk about golf. I am not a golfer, which they found hard to believe because England has so many beautiful golf courses which are not overcrowded like those in Japan. They told me that it was customary to dine early as many people who worked in Tokyo lived outside the city and sometimes had to take train journeys of one and a half hours. They preferred to catch a train about 21:00. It seemed that some executives were assigned dinner business entertaining, and others without commuting problems did the nightclub round of business entertaining. The food was excellent and everyone tried to be sociable, but the going was heavy, as they refused to discuss the interest we had in common – Kawasaki. We had a cognac and parted, with Mr. Ogawa telling me he would collect me at 9:00 the next morning. I slept well as the jet lag was gone, and the Burgundy had been heavy.

The following day there was a meeting with the three executives from the previous evening, as well as two more, both of whom were Directors of C. Itoh, Mr. Otani and Mr. Moto. This time I provided the audience and they talked very knowingly about the position of Kawasaki and the various matters that would have to be considered. Kawasaki was a giant company with a turnover in the hundreds of million dollar range. They manufactured all sorts of machinery, such as desalination plants, helicop-

49

ters, motor-cycles, printing machines, merchant and naval ships, and of course, VLCCs and turbines. In a new shipyard presently under construction at Sakaide, it would be possible to build six VLCCs per year. On the other hand, oil was very important to Japan, and Japan had no industrial ventures, or even many sales of large plant, such as desalination, in the Middle East. This market in Saudi Arabia was largely in American hands.

The fee they would earn to co-operate with AESA on turbine repairs and maintenance would be relatively insignificant, and unless there was spin-off in other directions for Kawasaki, they would not be interested. I said that it was not possible to promise that they could sell machinery and equipment, or obtain preferential oil if they co-operated in AGRY, but they must know that if they did a good job at AGRY, and had a presence in the Arabian Gulf, it would be bound to lead to other business in an economy which was expanding quickly and needed everything, and had the money to pay for it. I told them the decision must be theirs as I could hold out no bait beyond AGRY. If they were not interested, AGRY would not founder as another turbine manufacturer would be found, perhaps not so desirable. Both sides of the argument had been put, and the position was clear. C. Itoh said they would convey Kawasaki's answer to me in London.

I was driven back to the hotel and went to the travel agent in the shopping arcade to book a seat on a flight to Kuwait via Hong Kong and Bangkok for the next day. It had become my practice to obtain a Kuwait and Saudi Arabian visa before departing on any flight outside Europe, so I had no problem entering Kuwait, where again I had a room at the Sheraton. Whenever I spent a night away from Marcella, we always spoke on the telephone. This was easy from Tokyo, but now I settled down in my room in Kuwait to pass the three to four hours it took to get through to London and hear Marcella's voice at the other end of the telephone.

On the following day I walked to the offices of OAPEC to report on developments. Mr. Sadawi was becoming more interested in the project, and also more friendly. He had been born a Libyan and lived happily there until King Idris was overthrown by Colonel Gaddafi, when he went to Saudi Arabia. He was granted Saudi nationality and, like all converts, was more traditional than a native purist. As such he was suspicious of the possible disruptive factors which a large expatriate workforce would have on the Kingdom. He was the most difficult man to win over to the cause of AGRY. In the end he came to believe it was a constructive step forward, by which time we were on a first name basis.

An OAPEC Committee listened to the report about Kawasaki without comment, but seemed satisfied that some progress was being made. I was less sure. In the afternoon I flew to Riyadh. It being Thursday there were flights to the capital of the Kingdom; on Friday, the holy day of the week, flights were suspended. I stayed at the Yamama Hotel, which was on a par with the Kandarah Palace in Jeddah. The rooms had recently been repainted in cheerful colours and the bathrooms were new. I booked a telephone call to London, which I hoped would come through before midnight because as soon as Friday started, communications stopped. I also telephoned Maurice Brunel at his home. Maurice and his wife, Simone, had been long-time residents of Riyadh. He kindly offered to collect me the next morning for a sight-seeing tour around Riyadh and to a nearby oasis in the desert. I went to sleep – my London call did not come through.

I spent a very interesting day with Maurice and visited the original palace-fortress where King Abdul Aziz ibn Saud, in the beginning of the century, had overcome the Rashids and started to unite the tribes and form his Kingdom on the Arabian Peninsular. Maurice invited me to dinner at his home. Simone, who is French, prepared a delicious meal, while Maurice and I drank chilled lemonade and ate pistachio nuts which were imported in large quantities from the Lebanon. Maurice loved his work as consultant to Petromin and was a most objective, helpful source of information about Saudi Arabia and some of the people with whom I was likely to have dealings. He had a great admiration for Dr. Taher, and for Sheikh Yamani, with whom he had less contact. After dinner we drank coffee and Simone related some of her experiences in the souk. Riyadh has a huge souk. Simone told us that many of the Saudi princes would shop at the best jewellers in Paris, London and New York for costly necklaces, bracelets and rings for their wives. After a while the wives would tire of the jewellery and give some of it away to one or other of their maids. The maid would rush to the souk and sell it. Simone told of buying pieces from Cartier, Van Cleef and Boucheron, together with the original box, for 25 per cent of their value in Europe. The souk was a very exciting market for her.

I offered to walk back to my hotel, but Maurice wouldn't hear of it, saying it was much too dangerous. I couldn't imagine what the danger was, as surely there were no muggers in Riyadh. He then explained there were many wild dogs which had escaped from their owners, or had been released, and they now hunted in several large packs around the city at night; some of the dogs were thought to be rabid. We walked out to the car, which was parked in the driveway and surrounded by a high metal fence. Maurice started the car and drove to the gate, which was opened by an electronic device in the car. In the headlights I saw numerous dogs of all sizes, perhaps 20, barking and growling. They ran away as the car drove out and the gate closed behind it. Later, the authorities in Riyadh engaged the services of a European company to come and destroy the dogs humanely, but not before an English lawyer friend of mine had been badly bitten on both legs. He had left his hotel to go for a walk one evening and was set upon by the dogs. He managed to escape by climbing over a fence into a garden. He received treatment locally and had his wounds dressed, but flew back to London the next day. He told me that the worst period was waiting for the results of the tests to determine if he had rabies. Nobody ever walked at night in Riyadh. I was told that the phenomenon was peculiar to Riyadh and did not exist in any other city in the Kingdom.

The next morning, Saturday, I met Dr. Taher in the Petromin headquarters and brought him up to date about Japan. He was non-committal, although I sensed some impatience that everything was taking so long to arrange. On Sunday I flew to Jeddah and on to London. After two days at home I went to Madrid to see AESA and Fernando Azqueta to discuss the meeting with Kawasaki. There was really nothing to report, other than that a meeting had taken place, and that Kawasaki were briefed about the role we were hoping they would fulfil. Then for several weeks I waited to hear from Kawasaki, either directly or through C. Itoh, but there was no news. I met Mr. Iseki again, but on each occasion it was in connection with business he was proposing C. Itoh should do with Saudi Arabia. He didn't believe my protestations that my remit was exclusively in connection with AGRY. At each meeting Mr. Iseki informed me that no indication had yet been received from Kawasaki.

Dr. Taher's impatience was starting to transfer to me, and I decided on Saturday that I would fly back to Tokyo, together with Marcella. We flew JAL (Japan Airlines), and when the aircraft landed at Moscow Airport, went to the intourist shop and bought a jar of caviar which we had with our breakfast flying over Siberia. After clearing formalities at Tokyo Airport, we found a C. Itoh car waiting, which took us to the Okura Hotel (without our telling the driver our destination – Japan's excellent business information service!). The Okura was a delight, and in our opinion Tokyo's most attractive hotel. After unpacking we went downstairs and wandered through the shopping arcade, which was just as large and varied as at the Imperial Hotel. We selected a Japanese restaurant for dinner. Marcella was not even slightly jet-lagged, although I was feeling the eight-hour time difference. We sat at a table, in the middle of which was a gas ring fed by a cylinder of LP-gas under the table. All of the dishes were served in metal pots which were put on the ring to be kept hot – tempura, suki yaki and green tea, which we found had the same stimulating effect as coffee.

The next morning a C. Itoh car collected me for a meeting at their office. Marcella had a heavy schedule of museum visiting. She went first to the museums to polish her eye, and then to the antiquarians. Of particular interest were the eighteenth- and nineteenth-century screens, either in gold with chrysanthemums and forest scenes, or better still, the pale ones with a character of stark calligraphy brushed on by a master from the Edo period.

At the office of C. Itoh I asked for news of Kawasaki's decision and was told that a further meeting with Itoh and Kawasaki had been arranged for the next day as there were questions Kawasaki wanted to ask. We lunched with Mr. Itoh, the grandson of the founder of the firm and its present Chairman. It was clear that C. Itoh were very keen to do business in the Arabian Gulf, and saw AGRY as the lever to do this. They were keen for Kawasaki to join the management of AGRY, from which they were sure benefits would come to their trading company. This made Itoh a good ally of the project. After lunch I returned to the hotel and waited for Marcella. We had a good dinner at a Tempura bar in the Ginza district (area of restaurants and night clubs). Marcella described the beauty of things she had seen in three museums. She found the prices of good screens in Tokyo considerably higher than in London. We were told that this was down to the rising income of the Japanese, who were now keen importers of Japanese antiquities from all over the world, and that most of the Tokyo dealers had bought their stock in part at Christie's or Sotheby's Oriental Sales in London.

After dinner we decided to walk back to the hotel – we had watched the route taken by the taxi driver and felt we could follow it in reverse. We arrived back at the hotel and were ready for a good sleep, which I always found difficult after arriving in Tokyo from Europe without taking a pill; I wanted to be alert for the Kawasaki meeting and was pleased I didn't need one.

As previously there were the Kawasaki team players on one side of the table, but this time I was supported by four C. Itoh members. The gist of the discussion, which was opened by Kawasaki, was that, in principle, they were interested in providing turbine and technical expertise for a shipyard in the Arabian Gulf, and they would be pleased to co-operate with their old friends AESA, but it would be very difficult for them to provide the workforce of technicians we required for the following reasons. Japanese engineers, with whom they had raised the matter, refused to go out to the Arabian Gulf and stay there for long periods on a bachelor status. Those who had school-age children were unwilling to take them to the Gulf because the educational system in Japan was so competitive that if a child missed a year's schooling, it had literally no chance of passing entrance examinations into a University. They could not imagine that AGRY would provide a Japanese school in the way Aramco had provided an American one for children of its much larger workforce. On the other hand, Kawasaki, under the leadership of Mr. Kawakami, was trying to establish some kind of rota system where engineers would go out for three-month periods without their family, and then return to Japan. He believed that the cost would be less, even with the four annual round trip flights, than to establish an engineer and family in housing at AGRY. The bachelor engineers could live in a kind of

barracks. It was disclosed that Kawasaki were keen to establish a maintenance depot for their turbines and gears in the Arabian Gulf as a service
to their customers. This was not available from their competitors. Toshio
Kawakami explained that from Kawasaki's point of view, the AGRY project
had pluses and minuses and no decision had yet been reached.

Dr. Yoshida asked if I could find a bonus which would make that
decision easier, such as business of a different nature with Petromin or
OAPEC. Again, I had to discourage this thinking, and repeated that their
decision on AGRY must be taken on its own merit. I then suggested that
it might make reaching a decision easier for them if I could persuade
AESA to come to Tokyo, where the matter could be discussed jointly by
the two proposed participants, and if some agreement on AGRY was
reached, we could fly together to the Arabian Gulf. Kawasaki thought
this was a good idea, and as the year was drawing to a close, proposed
that I try to organize it for early in the New Year.

The meeting terminated with another lunch, this time at the Chinese
restaurant on the top floor of the World Trade Centre Building. It was
the best Chinese food I have ever eaten. There were six of us, Dr. Yoshida,
Mr. Hasegawa, Mr. Kawakami, Mr. Kakizawa and Mr. Kai from C. Itoh,
and myself. We sat at a large round table, in the centre of which was a
three-tiered, rotating wooden platform (in England called a 'lazy Susan'),
on to which waiters kept placing various dishes of Chinese food, and the
diners kept rotating the tiers, selecting portions from each. There was an
enormous amount of food and varieties which I had never before tried.
Although the meeting with Kawasaki was by no means conclusive, we
were getting to know each other better, and I believed Saudi Arabia
represented a tremendous temptation for them.

After lunch C. Itoh drove me back to the Okura and said that Marcella
and I were invited to their guest house for a traditional Japanese dinner.
The car would collect us at 18:30. There was no question of declining,
which would have caused great loss of face.

When we arrived at the guest house that evening we had to take off
our shoes and proceed in stockinged feet to a screened-off area – as I
took off my shoes, I was happy to notice several shoe horns hanging from
a rack. Marcella and I were greeted by Mr. Kai, Mr. Kakizawa and Mr.
Kawabe (the person from the 'plane at Jeddah who had introduced me
to C. Itoh in London). We sat cross-legged around a low table and
were served a continuous succession of small bowls containing traditional
Japanese delicacies. There were two geishas who brought our food, and
with each course would remark, 'This is xxx (a Japanese name), which
woodcutter wife give her man when he come home from cold forest',
etc. One of the geishas asked Marcella if she had dyed her hair black
because she was coming to Japan. Marcella explained that black was her
natural hair colour. 'I thought all English girls blonde', said our kind

geisha, and Marcella explained that she was Italian. Afterwards the other geisha played a plaintive melody on an instrument which resembled a one-string guitar. It was a very pleasant evening, with saki and much merriment.

At the close of the evening, Mr. Kai gave Marcella a beautiful bolt of white and gold brocaded silk. We said our thank yous and goodnights at the appropriate time (probably regulated by trains), and were driven back to the Okura. The young C. Itoh official who accompanied us in the car made the astonishing remark, pointing to the bolt of silk, 'Very expensive gift, be sure write letter thank you to Mr. Kai.' He was obviously unsure of the manners of Westerners.

In the morning, as nothing had been planned in the way of meetings, we took the fast 'bullet' train to the city of Kyoto. It was a comprehensive reminder of ancient Japan, with temples, bells and Buddhas. We packed that evening in readiness for an early departure to Hong Kong the following morning. We arrived at Hong Kong Airport around 14:00. The last fifteen minutes of the aircraft's approach was over sea, dotted with islands. Entering the traffic pattern to land, the aircraft appeared to approach tall buildings too closely which, on second sight, were tenements surrounding the airport. It let down as though into the midst of them. It was largely an illusion, as Hong Kong Airport is a safe one, even if it doesn't seem so from the cabin of a 747. The officials, men and women, of the immigration and customs services I thought were much better looking Asiatics than the Japanese. They were predominantly of Chinese blood, but with some Malaysian. Very quickly our bags were cleared and we got into a Rolls Royce with Mandarin Hotel painted on it in gold. The airport is in Kowloon, on the mainland, and we drove for about five minutes to the ferry port to cross over to Hong Kong on a ferry carrying cars, bicycles, pedestrians, chicken crates, rickshaws, and a lot more. There was room for seven other cars, which were quickly loaded. (Now a tunnel has been built, which is drab concrete, offering no view of the Hong Kong skyline and the colourful traffic of its waterway.)

Having travelled extensively in America and Europe, staying in renowned hotels, Marcella and I at once realized that the Mandarin ranked higher. The vast lobby was decorated in red lacquer, with frequent groupings of carved Chinese scenes painted in gold. There was a surplus of labour, and to service each room were valet, laundress, shoe-black and waiter. I changed shirt and suit on arrival in the room before going down to walk around Hong Kong; two hours later, on returning to the room before dinner, I found the shirt laundered and the suit pressed and hanging in the cupboard – this without asking.

I did not find walking around Hong Kong very interesting, as the pedestrian is confined to walking in the canyon space between very tall buildings which have sprung up on every available square metre of space, even encroaching the sidewalks. Any shopping, or bargain hunting, is done on the vast mezzanine floor of the hotels, with their many jewellery shops, tailors, shoe-makers, perfumeries, shirt-makers, camera and electronic shops, and all sorts of exotica in jade, lapis, carved wood and ivory. Although there is great quality amongst the more important jewellery shops, the whole gave us an impression of a giant, expensive Woolworth's. One can have a suit tailor-made in 48 hours, but the standard is not great.

That evening we took a taxi to the lagoon, where two large junks contain Chinese restaurants. On alighting from the taxi, one steps into a small tender and is quickly rowed out to one or other of the junks. The restaurants are very popular and the food is quite good, but much less appetizingly presented than at the Mandarin, where we had dinner the following night. In the morning the hotel provided a car and we were driven to see the view from the top of the exclusive 'hill' where all of the prestigious Hong Kong shipowners, bankers and traders, as well as the more important foreigners, have their homes. We also went to Repulse Bay, where we had a drink in a rambling English colonial hotel, and then on to Aberdeen and the junk community, where hundreds of sailing junks are tried up, with sides scraping, and whole families, together with chickens, cats and dogs, live on board. Perhaps they are used for fishing, or perhaps they provide houses for people who go off to work in Hong Kong. Here was poverty, certainly, but not, I concluded, the misery of India.

We returned to the Mandarin, had drinks in the attractive bar on the roof top, and enjoyed an excellent Chinese dinner. We were ready to move on the next morning. We had seen all there was to see of Hong Kong, and, pleasing as it was, there was an awareness of only a surface, with no depth visible. There was a feeling that if one tried to penetrate into the depth, it would contain unpleasant aspects far from the mild, smiling, exterior covering. I was to return at least a dozen more times on business, and never discovered anything more than, or different from, what we had found on that first visit.

# 7

# DECEMBER 1970 – MAY 1971

We flew to Delhi where we arrived at an almost empty airport at night. On leaving the terminal we could not find a taxi, but after about 15 minutes one turned up – it looked like a Vanguard, manufactured in England in the fifties. It was built in India, and possibly its manufacturer had bought all the tools and dies from the Standard Motor Company. The driver was wrapped in a blanket, and seemed very sleepy. He took us to our hotel, which was old and rambling, clean but in need of repair. The Ashoka had been one of India's best hotels during the British Raj. Four hours later, one of the same type cars and driver took us to Agra. What a fascinating two-hour drive. The road was long and straight, over a flat plain with scant vegetation on either side, although we saw some orange groves. We passed beggars, performing bears and their keepers, painted elephants, school children in neat uniforms, shrines and temples. At last we arrived in Agra and wandered around the town. We were offered antique stone carvings from some temple, but the taxi driver kindly warned us not to buy them because we would be prohibited from taking them out of India. We had a curry lunch at the Taj Mahal Hotel. A four-piece orchestra played 'Les feuilles mortes' in a very British two-step way, and the waiters wore starched red napkins on their heads, turban fashion, with an end sticking up like a cockscomb.

We visited the Taj Mahal. On this occasion realization lived up to expectation. It is a magnificent, delicate memorial of Mogul architecture. We also took in the red fort, which I found impressively solid. We were dismayed by the many beggars making a meagre livelihood by displaying their deformities, mostly the result of malnutrition. These sights are so much part of India, but it would not be easy to become inured and indifferent to them.

On the return to Delhi we drove through the dusk. There seemed to be fog as we approached the city and I asked the driver about it, surprised to find fog in so dry a climate. He said it wasn't fog, but smoke from the cooking fires of people camped in the fields on either side of the road. It wasn't necessary to spend another night in Delhi and early on Saturday morning we caught a Qantas flight to London. It had been a quick and interesting excursion, but AGRY had not been far from mind. It was still a long way away and I was forced to wait on Japanese and Spanish decisions.

On Wednesday, having recovered from jet-lag, I was in Madrid with AESA. I gave a résumé of the discussions with both Kawasaki and Itoh, and suggested the next step would be a meeting between AESA and Kawasaki. The first reaction was that Kawasaki would be welcome in Madrid, but I explained it would not be possible to get Dr. Yoshida and Mr. Hasegawa to Madrid on an exploratory meeting, even if Mr. Kawakami was willing. If we wanted the meeting to be decisive, it would have to take place in the presence of Dr. Yoshida and Mr. Hasegawa, which meant going to Tokyo. They agreed to accompany me in the New Year. It suddenly struck me, years were passing. About the same time last year I had got AESA to the Arabian Gulf, and in twelve months there had been so little progress, although so much had been spoken and written about AGRY.

Suspicions began to form about the Spanish not being really interested in the project, but at the same time not wanting to let it go. Up to now they had a valid reason for not committing themselves to the management contract, as the function would not be complete without a turbine specialist. Soon there would be a meeting with Kawasaki, and if that company was interested, AESA would have to declare itself.

In December I made one more visit to Madrid to try and fix the date for the AESA trip to Tokyo. Diaries were consulted, and the earliest mutually convenient date was departure for Tokyo on 20 February 1971. I informed Kawasaki when to expect us, and once more it was a question of waiting. Dr. Taher was in London on 13 December and telephoned me. He came to lunch the following day. Different from most Arabs, he liked steak, preferring a large sirloin to roast lamb. Maybe this was a consequence of his long exposure to the American way of life while studying for his doctorate in California. We ate steak and talked very candidly about the dry dock. He told me that some friends in different oil companies had told him they thought the Arabian Gulf dry dock was a good idea. He seemed to need to know if I still thought so. My opinion was still that the dry dock would become a credit to its Arab backers, but I confided that I was not yet certain we had the right management team, without which the dry dock would be a fiasco. I explained that I had the utmost belief in Kawasaki, which was a giant, efficient, publicly owned Japanese company, full of know-how, hard working and pragmatic, but that I was having doubts about AESA, which was a grouping of large Spanish shipyards, government-funded and government-owned. They built good VLCC hulls, Spanish workers were more industrious and loyal to their company than many in the UK, and they could provide a serious hard-working labour force for the dry dock, but the AESA Board and management structure was a typical government edifice, not to be compared with private enterprise like Kawasaki. AESA's typical government (plus the Spanish 'mañana' mentality) made me believe that they would take a very long time to reach a decision. I also got the impression that they hoped it might lead to some oil deal. Dr. Taher's blunt reaction was an 'Impossible'. He asked me why I didn't offer the management to Kawasaki alone. I explained about the Japanese not being able to find 1,200 to 1,500 men who would move out to the Arabian Gulf on a bachelor status, or if they came with family, to sacrifice their children's education. I also pointed out that the dry dock was intended to serve as a technical institute where young Arab Nationals would be taught all the skills so as to enable the dry dock to be Arabized within ten years of operation. The Japanese were probably good teachers, but only a few of the senior personnel spoke understandable English, and it was likely that the technical educational function of the dry dock would not be achieved.

Dr. Taher told me to come to Kuwait to attend an OAPEC Ministerial Meeting in a fortnight's time on 26 December, as probably the Committee would wish to ask me about the latest position of the dry dock. I had a growing respect for this intelligent, no-nonsense man, who inspired trust and loyalty.

On 23 December I flew to Kuwait where I met Maurice and Simone Brunel at the Sheraton. The next day I went over to the OAPEC office and talked with the permanent staff about the dry dock. For over two years perhaps no other person in the world had thought so much about an Arabian Gulf dry dock; I had become an expert on most arguments about its merit. So much information had been gleaned over the period from having talked with a variety of professionals and potential users. One disappointing fact I had learned was that as shipbuilding or repairing were labour-intensive industries, unions pushing up wages removed the possibility of shipyards paying their way without government subsidy. I always took pains to stress this point with OAPEC, pointing out that they must not look to the dry dock as a money-maker. It had other attributes. It would become an initial major step towards industrialization. It would be a prestige national facility, establishing the Arab world as being able to provide technical services, and removing the long stigma of an economy based on the single talent of oil production.

The next day was Friday – the Arab Sunday – but it was Christmas for the Brunels and me. The Sheraton did it very well, and the restaurant was filled with expatriate oil men and their wives from BP and Shell. Kuwait, like Saudi Arabia, was dry, but somehow the Sheraton managed to serve whisky in a tea pot. Even drunk from a cup, it was welcome, and added to the evening. There was a large Christmas tree in the lobby, hung with the usual decorations, all of which had been flown in from Germany.

The next day, Saturday, was the OAPEC Ministerial Conference. I shook hands with Sheikh Yamani and afterwards heard from him that the Conference had been unanimous in wanting the dry dock project investigation to continue. On Boxing Day there was further discussion on the dry dock, and I was questioned by the Committee. I got the feeling that they were not frustrated by the delays, rather it gave them time for cautious consideration before engaging in a venture which would cost more than $100 million. On Sunday 27 I flew back to London. Marcella and I spent New Year's Eve at Annabel's.

On 7 January 1971 Mr. Iseki and Mr. Masuda came to lunch at home. I was hoping to learn news of Kawasaki's reaction to the proposed AESA visit to Tokyo in February. Mr. Iseki said that Kawasaki was 'somewhat' interested in the project and that the 'Spanish people' would find that some preliminary work had been done. To my surprise, Mr. Iseki then asked if we couldn't do some 'easier' business between Saudi Arabia and Japan. I laughed, as that always seemed the first friendly response to blunt, abrupt, Japanese questions, and it softened the 'no' which was the reply. The Japanese reminded me of that well-known story about the fellow who kept on asking, because sometimes he got 'yes' for an answer. Dealing with Japanese traders was very different from dealing with their manufacturing companies. I thought that for a sophisticated, successful people, their approach seemed somewhat primitive. But this was perhaps not due to semantics, but communication in general. Rarely have I heard a Japanese observe in speech the politeness of their bows and the courtesy of their way of life. I believe this problem was fundamental, not only when they spoke a foreign language, but even when talking among themselves in Japanese. They were certainly intelligent and hard-working. Mr. Kawakami and I once flew together from Tokyo to London; during almost the whole flight he was writing in a notebook, the pages of which he completed with text and calculations taken from his mini computer, except for about half an hour, when he pushed his seat back into a horizontal position and dropped off to sleep. He awoke quite refreshed and resumed his task.

The day after my meeting with C. Itoh, I flew to Madrid for a meeting with AESA, in which I hoped to inspire Mr. Del Molino to do some preparatory work to show Kawasaki additional to the designs, lay-out and costings of SENER. Instead, I learned of AESA's misgivings about the project on religious grounds. They had learned that Saudi Arabia permitted no form of worship except Islam. Mr. Del Molino did not believe a large Spanish workforce and their families would be happy unless they could practise their Catholic faith. He pointed out that Muslims could worship in Spain, where Mosques had existed since the tenth century. I told him that religious restrictions applied only to Saudi Arabia, and AGRY might be located in Bahrain or Dubai, where more liberal religious views were held. More and more I was beginning to doubt AESA's intention to provide management for AGRY. I would have preferred being informed of this outright, so that I could resume looking for potential managers. Perhaps they held back still hoping for some oil-related business to be offered as an incentive, but I did not wish to provoke AESA's withdrawal, at least until after the Kawasaki meeting, in case something positive should transpire in Tokyo.

Back in London I began to prepare an evaluation of the situation for Dr. Taher, who always liked to know the bad news as quickly as the good. It became apparent that the major stumbling-block was the provision of a homogeneous workforce, and I began to wonder if divisional managers down to foremen level, could be provided from a prestigious shipyard to give shipowners confidence, and from foremen down to unskilled labour, from Pakistan or other Muslim country. If Pakistanis were less efficient than Europeans or Japanese, two Pakistanis would still cost less than one European. This was suggested to Dr. Taher in my report.

Admiral John Scotland had left UCS after its dissolution. He knew ships, shipyards and the Arabian Gulf. I engaged his help to draw up an optimum organization chart for AGRY, assuming that it should be capable of working two full shifts. This was ready for me to take to Tokyo.

Mr. Kawakami telephoned me requesting that I meet Mr. Katsumine from the Kawasaki London office. Mr. Katsumine came to Madrid for my meeting with AESA so that he could brief the Tokyo head office of the position before the visit to AESA and myself. Fernando Azqueta had telephoned me in London to say that he urgently wanted to talk about what he described over the telephone as a very important matter which he thought would help AESA to decide. Fernando and I dined together at the Jockey Club. He seemed hesitant to commence talking about the 'important' subject. However, he was bubbling, and we did not have to wait for coffee. Fernando said that he was building a VLCC at AESA which would be the flagship of his fleet. It would be the largest ship under the Spanish flag and was chartered to the Spanish National Oil Company, Hispanoil. He asked me to convey his invitation to Mrs. Yamani to launch the ship, explaining that this could possibly bring relations between AESA and Saudi Arabia forward. He was such a splendid chap, and a good friend, that I hated to spoil his fantasy. I had to tell him that unfortunately Sheikh Yamani was separated from his wife and lived a bachelor life in the Yamama Hotel in Riyadh. In any case, as Minister of the King, he could not appear to favour one European nation or its National Oil Company. The only official customer for Saudi Arabian oil was Aramco, and its shareholders Exxon, Mobil, Texaco and Chevron.

I asked Fernando's help in making it clear to AESA and its Spanish

61

government owners, that AGRY must be considered in isolation from any benefits to Spain inherent in the management contract, or not at all. Fernando understood the position, and I am sure made it clear to Claudio Abada, the AESA Chairman. I expected this might bring AESA's decision to a negative conclusion, but apparently not, as talks continued with AESA and Mr. Katsumine the following day. Mr. Katsumine was very positive and made a number of constructive suggestions for additional revenue which AGRY might earn through so-called 'planned maintenance contracts' whereby each VLCC equipped with Kawasaki turbines, gears, pumps, etc., would be logged in the Kawasaki computer in Tokyo and would receive regular maintenance and replacements at each AGRY docking.

I flew to Paris from Madrid to meet a French VLCC shipbuilder I knew, Chantiers Atlantique. We had a pleasant general discussion about finding management, during which Mr. Charron gave his opinion that Frenchmen would not be eager to leave home to work in the Arabian Gulf for whatever wages.

On 10 February I flew to Riyadh to see Dr. Taher before the Tokyo visit. We discussed the concept of the managing yard's own personnel being provided, from divisional managers to foremen, with skilled and unskilled labour recruited from the Indian subcontinent. He agreed with this, providing the managers selected would be responsible, in their contract, for the work carried out by the Pakistanis or others. We lunched at his home and I met Mrs. Taher and their daughter Nashua, who at five spoke good English. Khalid and Tarik, their sons, were at school and did not come home for lunch. He said the whole family enjoyed the boat which had been sent out from England, but he could not teach the boys how to waterski as he did not know how to do it himself. Dr. Taher was planning to send the boys to London in the summer, to improve their English, and asked if I could arrange for them to learn how to waterski.

I returned to London feeling that the rules concerning the managers providing a homogenous work force had been relaxed. This should make it easier and less costly to man AGRY.

On Saturday, 20 February, Del Molino, Asophros and I met at London Airport and took the JAL flight over Moscow to Tokyo, where we were met by Mr. Kawakami on Sunday morning and driven to the Hotel Okura. Toshio Kawakami gave Del Molino and Asophros a very comprehensive study on AGRY which he had compiled. It included a complete organization chart showing responsibilities of AESA and KHI (as Kawasaki Heavy Industries were known internationally). It had been based on SENER layouts and was the professional job which such an experienced group could produce. Del Molino and Asophros were impressed and took their copies to study in preparation for the next day's meeting at the KHI office.

I had not slept on the flight and was tired, stiff and jittery. By the telephone was a card giving the number of the hotel massage service, with a little phrase printed on it 'good for jet-lag'. I dialled the number and someone said, 'How can I help you?' I asked whether it was possible to have a message, and the man's voice replied, 'Right away sir, room number please.' After about five minutes, the doorbell rang, and when I opened it, standing there was a small, slim, Japanese woman in her sixties, wearing a kimono. She had a thin mattress rolled up under her arm, which she put on the floor and said, 'Lie on, no pyjamas, please.' Then, for more than half an hour, she walked all over me with bare feet, front and back. When she had finished she said, 'In bed,' and went to the door to let herself out, saying, 'You sleep now,' and I did. When I awoke ten hours later, it was 05:00 and I was very hungry. Room service brought me a large, excellent breakfast on a tastefully appointed tray, with two pots of coffee, one of which the waiter placed on a small hot-plate in the bathroom. I was rested, felt well, and had become an ardent believer in Japanese massage. The women had left so quickly there was not even time to tip her. In Japan, waiters, bellboys, and even taxi drivers, give the impression of not expecting a tip, perhaps that would be losing face. I never tried for a reaction to withholding a tip because the service was always so good, without being servile, that it deserved recognition.

At 9:00 Del Molino, Asophros and I met downstairs near the front door, where there was a live cherry tree in bloom. The KHI car was punctual and took us to the World Trade Centre Building. The driver must have communicated with the office *en route*, because Toshio Kawakami was at the entrance to welcome us. Once more the KHI team were ranged on one side of the long table, with Del Molino, Asophros and myself on the other side. There was also a large blackboard. Toshio Kawasaki gave numbers, and indicated the responsibilities of the 28 KHI men which he considered would need to come to the Arabian Gulf on 90–day rotas and be capable of handling all the machinery repairs likely to be required. He said they would be backed up by a small team of skilled and semi-skilled workers from AESA. The meeting went well – in fact, too well, as both Del Molino and Asophros accepted all of the KHI suggestions. I had hoped for heated argument, and such remarks as, 'No, no, in Spain we don't do it like that', which would have been the case had they given serious thought to the co-ordinated management function. KHI also seemed disappointed, and the only argument arose between Mr. Kawakami and myself, in which I was proved wrong. We broke for lunch, again to the excellent Chinese restaurant on the top floor. Dr. Yoshida mentioned that Mr. Kawakami and three engineers would be joining the AESA representatives and me on Thursday to fly to the Arabian Gulf. This was something quite new, and was an excellent idea, except that neither Del Molino nor Asophros had Saudi Arabian visas. The AESA representatives said it was not possible for them to go to the

Gulf on this occasion, as both had to return to Spain. Nothing more was said then, and I did not know if Mr. Kawakami planned to go with his team in any case.

After lunch we were driven back to to Okura. A further meeting was scheduled for the following day to discuss the time-table for mobilization in terms of months after the OAPEC decision was taken to proceed with AGRY. The workforce should be on site at least during part of the building time of AGRY, rather than move in when in when it was complete. The Japanese seemed so much more energetic and positive about the project, I started to wonder how well they would be able to work under the Spanish. It had been decided that a management company would be formed which would receive a fee from the OAPEC owners. It would be responsible for all the management duties. That company, it was suggested, would be owned 60 per cent by AESA and 40 per cent by KHI, with each company putting up some form of performance bond in respect to the fulfilment of their specific activities.

That evening C. Itoh invited Del Molino, Asophros and me to dinner in a Japanese-style restaurant in the Okasaka district of Tokyo. It was very enjoyable hospitality, after which we were taken to a night club which turned out to be a Western-style 'girlie' show, with additional Japanese crudities that would not have passed censorship in the West. We were eventually sent home in the Itoh car, and our hosts said they would make their own way.

Next day at the KHI meeting I disclosed that Dr. Taher would accept a homogenous workforce from Spain down to foreman level, with skilled and unskilled labour recruited from Pakistan or another Muslim state. AESA felt this made matters easier, as it would greatly reduce the number of personnel they would have to provide. The Japanese, slow to start, were now keen to get going, and tried to extract a decision from AESA, but this was a matter for the Board in Spain.

That night I invited Toshio Kawakami to dinner, as Del Molino and Asophros had some friends they were planning to meet. I asked Mr. Kawakami whether KHI would take over the full management role, down to foreman level, and was told that in no way would this be possible, or even advisable, as the necessary continuity could not be maintained on a rota basis, with key personnel coming and going every 90 days. He was equally candid, and asked whether it was possible to find some other European shipyard. I told him of the previous experience with UCS and Swan Hunter, but made it clear that if AESA dropped out, every effort would be made to find another yard. There was a further meeting the following day in which C. Itoh representatives were also included. It was now clear that progress depended on a decision by AESA, and regrettably this was not in the hands of Del Molino or Asophros. This time C. Itoh were our hosts at lunch. Everyone was working on Del Molino and

Asophros, giving them arguments to use with their Board. KHI had declared itself keen to proceed. The AESA representatives departed for Madrid, and I for London. On the aircraft it became clear to me that I had to force the issue with AESA. An ultimatum must be given, as too much time was being lost, and possibly credibility also, as we were still unable to nominate managers after about a two-year search.

Two days after I returned to London, Maurice Brunel telephoned me from Geneva. I flew over to meet him and over dinner I disclosed that I felt the AESA Board were dragging their feet and would ultimately turn down the management. Maurice said something should be done, lest OAPEC lose patience with the project – exactly my own fear. The following day I once again checked into the Hotel Ritz in Madrid. It was 2 March and the sun shone; it was a beautiful spring-like day. That night Jacobo Valdes and Del Molino joined me for dinner. I told them OAPEC was getting impatient, and either AESA was prepared to join the AGRY venture, or I would be instructed to look for another manager. Jacobo Valdes said he could understand OAPEC's attitude, and told Del Molino that in his view it was time to get a statement of interest from the AESA Board. Del Molino undertook to talk to his directors as soon as possible to pry an answer from them. Under General Franco, government-owned enterprises were reluctant to take any major decisions. It was safer not to make a mistake than to strive for progress.

Back in London I telephoned Toshio Kawakami in Tokyo and informed him about the meeting with Del Molino. Kawakami said he would try to come to Madrid to meet formally the AESA directors involved, and would be in a position to speak on behalf of KHI's willingness to share in the management of AGRY. He said he would communicate directly with AESA and advise me the date of the meeting in Madrid. I learned this was to take place in three weeks' time on 23 March.

In the mean time, Mr. Jamal Jawa, the Deputy Governor of Petromin, came to London and asked to be brought up to date with developments relating to the impending KHI/AESA meeting. Toshio Kawakami had taken positive action. It was characteristic of his nature (during the Second World War he had been a test captain on the suicide (kamikaze) two-man submarines which KHI built). He was intelligent, and also resourceful in his AGRY work, and I was very pleased to have him on the project. We all gathered in Madrid on 23 March at the offices of AESA. Arias, Del Molino, Jacobo Valdes, Toshio Kawakami, and Mr. Ishige, a KHI planner. The meeting was a long one, during which AESA openly admitted that they had as yet been unable to reach a decision about performing their part of the management role. They said there was much in the project which appealed to them and, then again, they saw large problems, not in connection with the operation of AGRY, but in providing the manpower on a continuous basis for at least ten years as OAPEC required. They were relieved that the numbers had been reduced, with the requirement only to provide personnel of foreman level and above. A ten-year commitment was a long one in the world of shipbuilding and ship-repairing. It was agreed that AESA and SENER would join KHI to visit Dammam and Bahrain in mid-April, after which AESA would reach their decision. Kawakami, Ishige and I remained in Madrid a further two days for discussions with SENER about their lay-out of AGRY. Afterwards KHI and I went to Bilbao to see the head office and design centre of SENER. We had dinner with Don Fernando Asqueta at the Yacht Club, of which he was commodore. AESA arranged a visit to their large Bilbao yard, where they were building Fernando Azqueta's VLCC. On the Friday we flew back to London, from where the two KHI representatives took a flight to Tokyo.

The following Monday I flew to Riyadh to meet Dr. Taher and advise him of the joint visit planned for mid-April. It was gratifying that neither Sheikh Yamani nor Dr. Taher showed impatience at the slow progress. Dr. Taher was looking for possible ways of improving the cash flow. Unfortunately, I could not hold out any hope. Repair prices must be competitive in price and quality, and labour would be expensive. The best position one might achieve would be a break-even, or small profit, if no provision had to be made for amortization of the investment and the construction cost could appear as a government grant from OAPEC. If that was possible, then probably an operating profit would be achieved. The dry dock would never be rewarding financially, but the benefits were there in terms of technical training, industrialization and all the other arguments Dr. Taher had heard from me before. He said he was looking forward to meeting the Japanese and hearing their views after they had visited the two sites under consideration. We lunched together and I caught the afternoon flight to Jeddah and on to London. It was now possible to fly non-stop to London from Jeddah by VC10.

There were weeks ahead in which to consider the things which might frustrate the realization of AGRY, not the least of which that the OAPEC sponsors might get bored with the difficulties which kept arising in finding managers, and take that to mean that the dry dock just wasn't meant to be. I believed that as long as Sheikh Yamani continued to feel positively about the dry dock, OAPEC would follow, as they had such a respect for his wisdom.

I made some further cash flow projections based on KHI's very helpful study, complete with cost data. I had also obtained price lists from the agents of three VLCC repair yards operating in Europe – Verolme, Lisnave and Terrin. The cash flows were prepared in considerable detail. I sent these airfreight to Dr. Taher to give him some queries to raise with KHI and AESA when they met. Small operating profits without amortization were forecast, indicating that the dry dock would not require an annual subsidy. However, I still doubted that AESA would accept the management role, and I knew AGRY required managers very soon, or else the project stood a good chance of being dropped. Until AESA said no, it was impossible to initiate talks with any other shipyard. Those three months in 1971 – April, May and June – were the most taxing of the entire period of AGRY development.

In mid-1971 orders were placed for a number of tankers, each exceeding 300,000 DWT. These ships became known as ultra large crude carriers (ULCCs). There was even talk that eventually a tanker of 1 million tons carrying capacity would be built. A short time afterwards, Lisnave, the only purpose-built repair yard for giant tankers, announced that it was in fact considering building a dry dock to accommodate vessels up to 1 million DWT. Lisnave was a very new yard, built in the 1960s by Portugal's largest industrialist, Jose Manuel de Mello. Lisnave possessed two VLCC size dry docks, and the best location in Europe at Lisbon, which all ships, having discharged in North East Europe, would pass on the way to load in the Arabian Gulf. Mr. De Mello was interviewed by the shipping press about the 1 million ton dry dock, and one reporter asked him about AGRY, and whether Lisnave would be interested in managing it. Mr. de Mello replied, 'Certainly not, as we would be creating competition for our own yard by establishing and supporting a dry dock also in a very good location.'

Bigger and bigger ships began to be ordered. Shipowners saw the advantage of carrying an ever-increasing tonnage of oil, for which they were paid a rate per ton transported, while the operating cost of the ship remained substantially the same as for a vessel half the size. Orders for VLCCs and ULCCs were being contracted at about 90 per year, with too few dry docks to accommodate them. The need for AGRY increased with each big ship ordered.

Before proceeding to the Arabian Gulf, I flew to Madrid to discuss with SENER whether AGRY's planned size of accommodating up to a 250,000 DWT VLCC should be increased in view of the many orders being placed for larger ships. We agreed an optimum size dry dock, able to take the majority of big tankers, should have a capacity for a 350,000–400,000 DWT vessel. SENER made new calculations for the cost of lengthening and widening the dock. They were ready for me to take to the Gulf the following day. The additional cost was by no means pro rata to the size increase, and could be achieved for an extra $12 million. My recommendation would be to increase the size of AGRY to enable it to be suitable for almost all the big crude carriers.

I left Madrid for Beirut and spent the night at the wonderful old St. George's Hotel, which for decades had been the meeting place for all sorts of intrigants, from the big Levantine merchants dealing with the requirements and investments of the kings and rulers of the Arabian

Peninsular to Kim Philby, who used to sit on its large terrace overlooking the Mediterranean and drink his four double whiskies each evening. He was a regular fixture in the 1960s, and anyone needing him could always be sure to find him there. Beirut was, for a very few more years, the showcase of the Arab world.

It had been arranged that I would meet both the AESA and KHI representatives at Dhahran Airport on 20 April. I got to Dhahran the day before and was delighted to find that we were not booked into the old Airport Hotel, but instead were staying at a very comfortable new hotel, the Al Khobar Palace, in nearby Al Khobar. The town of Al Khobar owed its existence principally to supplying the requirements of the Aramco compound and its expatriate population. It had shops selling every imaginable consumer durable, fresh food of every kind, supermarkets, chemist shops, hi-fi and other electronic equipment. One saw and heard many Americans in the streets. It was near the main crude oil loading terminal at Ras Tanura and also the export refinery, about 20 miles from Dammam. The hotel and Al Khobar would give the SENER and AESA people a much more 'with it' impression than had their previous trip, and it would also reassure the Japanese.

After the arrival of both groups (Kawakami and Ishige from KHI, Del Molino from AESA, and Valdes and Serrano from SENER), we dined together at the hotel and planned our activities for the next two days. The next day both Dammam Pier and a proposed site in Bahrain would be visited, following which we would all fly to Riyadh and report to Dr. Taher.

The 21st was a long day, starting at first light, when we visited the Dammam Pier, flying at noon to Bahrain where the British Port Captain (Capt. Duck), took us by boat to two possible sites near the deep water channel. At 18:00 we flew back to Dhahran Airport and were driven to the hotel. Petromin had arranged re-entry visas or we could not have returned to Saudi Arabia the same day. Over dinner we discussed the investigations of the day. The unanimous opinion was that it would be considerably cheaper to build the dry dock at Dammam than Bahrain, but it would be easier to operate in Bahrain. After dinner the KHI and SENER representatives went off to do their calculations in preparation for their meeting the next day with Dr. Taher. AESA had produced a manning schedule showing that they would require 146 men at levels from foreman and above to carry out the hull work at AGRY. Del Molino said that this was a much more feasible number for them to provide.

Dr. Taher received us all at lunch in Riyadh and listened to reports from AESA, SENER and KHI. He asked Del Molino if his company had made up its mind. Del Molino said that with the reduced number of AESA people to be provided, he was hopeful that his management would agree. Dr. Taher, in his usual clear, pragmatic way outlined that first, he was agreed that the dry dock size should be increased to accept vessels up to 400,000 DWT; second, that SENER should calculate the cost of building the dock in both Dammam and Bahrain, so that OAPEC would have this input when they made their decision after managers had been found; third, that I should go to Kuwait and tell OAPEC about developments. After lunch we flew back to Dhahran and Al Khobar. The KHI, AESA and SENER representatives flew off next morning and I went to Kuwait for a meeting with OAPEC, who asked me to submit a written appreciation of the situation from London, as the secretariat wished to circulate it to member countries.

It was difficult to determine if there had been any progress, apart from the increase in size being agreed by Dr. Taher – in the event that AGRY was ever built! I had a nagging feeling that the situation was becoming confused with a choice of sites, still only half a management team, and, worst of all, I began to notice friction between the methodical Japanese and the more casual Spanish approaches. I wondered how well Japanese engineers would work for Spanish bosses. Although my inclination was to substitute the Spanish with a more enthusiastic group, I had no idea where another potential manager could be found. All VLCC shipyards were full of work and needed all their personnel down to foreman level. Even if a suitable shipyard existed, I could not approach them until AESA withdrew. Dr. Taher would not agree to dump them, as they had made their contribution. It was not Del Molino, but the AESA Board who were causing delays.

I sent my report to the OAPEC secretariat in the usual way, then flew to Bilbao for a talk with Don Fernando Azqueta, who always tried to be helpful, and was such a valuable interpreter of Spanish thinking. In Bilbao Fernando was cautious, pointing out that AESA had a full order book and were doing particularly well in their VLCC shipyards. At the present time, managing AGRY would be of fairly insignificant financial interest, unless there could be some oil-related inducement, which he now realized would not be possible. He went on to say that in those circumstances he did not believe AESA was interested, but he felt that their problem was saying no to Petromin, which AESA would be very reluctant to offend. I was sure Fernando had correctly appraised the situation. Now it became my problem to find a diplomatic way for them to decline their services to AGRY. I could not provoke such a matter without Dr. Taher's approval, and Dr. Taher would want to know who I had in mind to replace AESA.

On my return to London there was a cable from Dr. Taher requesting a meeting in Cairo the following Friday, 2 May. This could not have come at a better time. I flew to Cairo and stayed at the Nile Hilton, crossing the Nile to the Sheraton for lunch with Dr. Taher. After listening to the summary of the situation with AESA, Dr. Taher asked whether AESA

69

could perform if they agreed to join the management team. I said I believed they would be excellent technically, but that I had two reservations. The first was language, as not may Spaniards at foreman level spoke English, which was also true of the Japanese. I felt communications would be difficult and that some of the benefits of training young Arab Nationals would be lost if the Arab trainees could not understand their Spanish instructors. The second worry was that I did not believe the Japanese would work very smoothly under Spanish direction. AESA had insisted on 60 per cent control of the management company. Dr. Taher authorized me diplomatically to disengage from AESA, giving them a way out in which they would not feel they were being dismissed, and one where they would not consider their withdrawal had jeopardized future relations with Saudi Arabia. I undertook to try. Dr. Taher said it would be helpful to clarify the AESA position and obtain construction costs from SENER for the Dammam and Bahrain sites to report at the next OAPEC Ministerial Conference in Kuwait on 5 June.

I returned to London and then flew to Spain to meet SENER who were almost ready with the costings of a 400,000 DWT dry dock for both sites. That evening Fernando Del Molino and I dined together. I disclosed that on 5 June I would have to report on the AGRY status quo at a meeting in Kuwait and that I would be grateful if AESA could let me have their decision before 3 June. He began by telling me that the project was very interesting and appealed to him, but he was concerned at sending out so many Spanish technicians and managers with their families to a part of the world where they would have to hide their Catholic worship and could not attend a Catholic Church. This would be particularly difficult for the wives and mothers trying to bring up their children as good Catholics. He said he had been informed that in Saudi Arabia there would be a prohibition on Catholic priests holding services. He saw this as the major stumbling-block to AESA participation, and he promised to give me a definite answer prior to my departure for Kuwait. So far so good; what more reasonable withdrawal than on religious grounds outside the control of either party. I believed that I had been given AESA's answer and that they would withdraw. I returned to London to await official confirmation.

On Friday, 28 May Mr. De Molino telephoned me and asked whether I could come to Madrid for a meeting the following Monday. Abado, Del Molino and Arias received me in the AESA Boardroom and Claudio Abado said that with great reluctance AESA had to decline the opportunity of joining in the project. He spoke of possible union problems, about sending members of the shipbuilding union to work in Saudi Arabia where unions were against the law, and also mentioned the religious prohibitions which would represent real problems for a faithful Catholic. There were more cordialities and we all shook hands again, expressing mutual regret. AESA had been part of the team for over a year, and had made substantial contributions. After the meeting I went over to the SENER office. Jacobo Valdes said he was disappointed, but had anticipated AESA's decision. We both considered the loss of the potential managers a set-back, and hoped it would not discourage OAPEC when it was announced at the June meeting. Jacobo Valdes gave me the calculations on the Dammam and Bahrain sites to take to Kuwait.

I was back in London that evening, and now we were free to approach other shipyards for the management position, I began to make a list of all the probables: three in Sweden, one in Denmark, three in Germany, two in Holland and one in Belgium – all with VLCC experience, and all with English language fluency. I spoke first with the yards where I knew someone in authority. By the afternoon I had contacted all ten shipyards. They all knew of the AGRY project from the shipping press, but all ten shipyards said they were not interested in meeting to discuss their assuming a management responsibility. Some were very quick in declining, others took the time to speak of their full order books and needing all personnel to complete their new building programme. I would have to disclose to OAPEC that I had tried to find alternative managers and had been unsuccessful with all the obvious VLCC yards.

Strange as it might seem, I remained confident that I would find a manager. I knew I must be cautious in saying this to OAPEC after two years of effort and expense, lest they suspect me of misleading them. I looked forward to the OAPEC meeting. The key to the dry dock was Sheikh Yamani, and as long as he believed in it, everyone else from the other OAPEC countries would follow. It was always necessary to give Sheikh Yamani self-supported facts and never to exaggerate any of the benefits which might accrue from it. He is a very conservative man and preferred, I knew, a low profile presentation.

On Thursday evening, 3 June, I checked into the now familiar Kuwait Sheraton. On Friday, even though it was the holy day of the week, I met Abdul Aziz Al-Turki, Assistant Secretary General of OAPEC, and Jamal Jawa, Deputy Governor of Petromin. In our discussion we covered the fact that the size had increased to accommodate ships of 400,000 DWT, that the cost had also increased by $12 million, and that we had lost our managers on the hull side. No encouraging news of progress, but it was helpful to talk openly of these matters off the record.

I was not called to address the OAPEC Conference but after the meeting, on 6 June, Sheikh Yamani invited Dr. Taher and me to lunch. He told me that OAPEC wanted to continue with the dry dock pursuit and asked me if I was losing interest through all the problems. I assured him I was not, and fully believed in the merit of the project if all the pieces could be put together. Apparently, most of the discussion during the meeting had been about the price of oil, which was currently at around

71

$2.50 per barrel. The OAPEC members, all of whom (except Bahrain) were also OPEC members, felt the price should be increased. We were drinking Evian water with lunch; Sheikh Yamani pointed to the litre bottle and said that the cost of Evian water at the hotel was $1.00, but perhaps $0.50 when sold by the distributor. There were about 160 litres to a barrel of oil, which made Evian's price more than 30 times the price of oil, and Sheikh Yamani wondered which the world could more easily do without.

Dr. Taher and I met again later and he asked what I intended to do in the way of finding managers now that AESA had gone. I told him I had already tried the ten most suitable VLCC yards in Europe, and all of them had turned the dry dock management down. It might have sounded rash, but I told him I was sure that I would find the right managers. He mentioned he had to be in Tokyo the following month and proposed I meet him there so that we could jointly visit KHI. He also told me his two sons, Khalid and Tarik, would soon be in London to enrol in summer school at Rye, Sussex and he asked me if I would shop with them for whatever clothes they needed, and, if there was time, to have them taught how to waterski.

# 8

# JUNE – DECEMBER 1971

On 17 June I met Khalid and Tarik at London Airport. Khalid was then 13 and Tarik 11. Both boys spoke a little English. I put them up at No. 11 Cadogan Gardens, around the corner from my home. No. 11 is a well-known small hotel, with very comfortable rooms and baths, impeccably clean, and the best breakfast in London – the only meal they served. Many of my friends from the continent and America used it when visiting London privately and not on company expense accounts. Khalid and Tarik had dinner with us at home that evening. They were fledglings, very likeable, bright young Arab boys, keen to seek experience and learn everything. We have remained friends ever since. Khalid has married a Brazilian girl and Tarik a Californian.

The following morning we went shopping at Harrods to buy sports jackets and grey flannel trousers, that form the uniform of the English boarding school. After they were dressed in their new clothes, we went to the sports department and bought two rubber wet suits – the weather was too cold for someone coming from Saudi Arabia to go waterski-ing in just swimming shorts.

Khalid got up on his skis the first time, but Tarik, who wore glasses, had difficulties as the glasses kept getting wet and he could not see. The instructor asked him to take off his glasses, after which he was up and away after the first try. They spent a couple of hours practising and became quite comfortable on their skis. We took them to dinner that night at a Chinese restaurant and the following day they had another two hours' practice. On Saturday, to divert their preoccupation at attending a first boarding school, we went to the musical 'Hair' which had just opened in London. The boys loved the show and bought an LP of the music to take back to the Kingdom.

On Sunday Marcella and I drove Khalid and Tarik down to the school at Rye where they met the headmaster. There were boys at the school from a variety of European countries, but none Arabic speaking, which I thought would help them to concentrate on English. We left them looking solemn and a little uncertain and on Wednesday telephoned the school to learn that the boys were settling in well. I cabled this news to Dr. Taher.

The time of my departure for Tokyo on 2 July was getting nearer. I had a few meetings in London trying to pick up suggestions of which shipyards I might approach. One of the persons I spoke to was Tony Hepper, the former Chairman of UCS. It was a tough time to interest VLCC yards when they were all so busy with their new building orders, but we spoke of Vickers, and I had dealt with them in the 1950s when I was director of a shipping company which had built tankers there. I was hesitant to approach them just yet as they were not a VLCC yard, and OAPEC might object to them on that score. However, as far as prestige was concerned, none was greater, but I first had to clarify the situation with Dr. Taher.

On arrival in Tokyo, I was met by the KHI car and taken to the New Otani Hotel, which was Dr. Taher's favourite, situated in a very large Zen garden. Dr. Taher was coming to Japan to meet representatives of Chyoda, Mitsubishi's chemical division, about a refinery project that Petromin was considering. Before he arrived I had a meeting with KHI and C. Itoh. They worried about AESA's withdrawal and hoped I would be able to find a shipyard to replace them. It was going to be an important occasion for KHI to meet Dr. Taher and they arranged for their President, Mr. Yotsumoto, to receive him on Friday for a discussion, followed by lunch at the KHI guest house.

Together with Mitsubishi representatives, I met Dr. Taher at the airport. After checking into his hotel, Dr. Taher and I lunched at the roof top restaurant, which slowly revolved as we talked and ate. He asked about his sons and then enquired if I had yet found a manager. The direct answer of course was no, but I went on to tell him about Vickers. It was one of the world's most prestigious shipyards, although it was not a VLCC yard. The largest tanker Vickers had built was for BP, the *British Admiral* of 125,000 DWT. I explained that their limitation on size was due to a lock at Barrow-in-Furness, through which all ships built by Vickers had to pass on their way to the sea. The lock belonged to the River Authority which would not agree to its being altered. The Vickers yard was about 100 years old, but their output was very modern. In addition to building merchant shipping, they were the lead yard in the UK for building Polaris submarines, as well as cruisers, etc., for the Royal Navy. Vickers had international experience in managing shiprepair yards in India and Pakistan for both naval and merchant ships. I asked Dr. Taher whether I should go and see Vickers. He reminded me that he was acting as agent for the Minister, Sheikh Yamani, but that he would discuss it with him as soon as possible.

It was clear that Japan's biggest company held Dr. Taher and Petromin in high regard. That night Dr. Taher and I were collected by Mr. Tamima and driven to the Mitsubishi guest house where the company President and other notables received us. Until Dr. Taher explained that I was working with KHI (their competitor) on the OAPEC dry dock project and was a consultant to Petromin they were unable to identify me. I was pleased to hear them tell Dr. Taher that they had read of the OAPEC dry dock and were happy that Japan was involved. We were taken on a tour of the beautiful formal gardens surrounding the building and then were served drinks, after which we entered a large dining-room for a dinner which was light, in spite of twelve separate courses (i.e. the number served at ceremonial dinners). After some speeches we were driven back to the hotel.

The following day Dr. Taher spent in discussion with Chyoda, so I did not see him again until we were both collected on Friday by Toshio Kawakami and a KHI car to go to the World Trade Centre Building. The white-haired, distinguished KHI President Yotsumoto, the Executive Vice-President, Mr. Hasegawa, and the Managing Director, Dr. Yoshida, all extended their welcome to Dr. Taher. We then took our places around a table in the President's office. Mr. Yotsumoto made a short, well-worded speech informing Dr. Taher of the interest his company had in collaborating with Petromin in the fruition of the dry dock project. Dr. Taher replied, speaking about Petromin and OAPEC and the aims of the Arabian Gulf Arab oil-producing countries, to try to establish joint industrial ventures. Dr. Taher explained that if the dry dock could be achieved, it would be the first Pan-Arabic industrial project, and that the benefits derived from technological transfer would be spread to each of the OAPEC states through the young Arab engineers who would train at the facility. Dr. Yoshida said that KHI felt privileged to be a participant in such an inter-Arab prestige venture, and would do everything possible to realize it. Dr. Taher has a positive, forceful personality, which impresses people. (Although he probably would not have relished the comparison, his manner struck me as similar to that of Dr. Kissinger.) He certainly won friends at KHI. Dr. Yoshida asked him of what he was a doctor (economics), disclosing that his doctorate was in welding. Dr. Taher asked if KHI would undertake the management of the dry dock on their own. Dr. Yoshida explained that there were two reasons this was impossible. First, there was a VLCC shipbuilding boom, and KHI were now turning out eight VLCCs per year in the Sakaide yard and could not spare workers to send to the Gulf, apart from those engineers who would be sent to repair turbines, pumps, steering gear, and other VLCC machinery. These would not need to exceed 50 in number. He said the other reason was the one that Mr. Kawakami had already disclosed, which was the reluctance of a Japanese to go abroad with his family for even six months, because if a child missed just that short time away from the Japanese educational system, even with tutoring, it would be difficult to catch up to the standard acceptable for a place at a Japanese University. (Later, Dr. Taher told me he believed the first reason was the more important to KHI.)

Dr. Taher then told me to ask KHI about Vickers. I addressed the question to Dr. Yoshida, asking whether KHI would consider Vickers an acceptable and capable partner in the management of the dry dock, explaining that no contact had been made as yet with Vickers. Dr. Yoshida said, in a formal Japanese way, that indeed it would be an honour to co-operate with Vickers. He then added that Vickers had built Japan's first battleship, the 'Makassar', which had been launched at the Barrow-in-Furness yard in 1900. Dr. Yoshida and Toshio Kawakami offered to approach Vickers officially, but I said that, subject to Dr. Taher's view, I preferred to speak first with Sir Leonard Redshaw, Chairman of the Vickers Shipbuilding Group, whom I had known since 1951. Dr. Taher said that, in any case, he would have to obtain Sheikh Yamani's approval, as OAPEC had agreed a management contract only with a VLCC yard. Dr. Yoshida laughed and said VLCCs were playthings compared with the sophisticated vessels Vickers built.

Dr. Taher invited his KHI hosts to a luncheon party he was giving the following day at the Saudi Arabian Embassy before he left in the afternoon for San Francisco to attend an Aramco Board Meeting. Mr. Yotsumoto was unable to attend, but Dr. Yoshida, Mr. Hasegawa and Toshio Kawakami said they were delighted to accept. On our way back to the hotel, I asked Dr. Taher whether we should have mentioned that Mitsubishi would also be at the lunch. He told me that Japan had a different concept of competition than existed in the West. When MITI (The Ministry of International Trade & Industry) was informed that one major Japanese industry was involved on a project, its competitors were told to 'lay off'. I would never be able to get Mitsubishi interested in the dry dock project for their shipbuilding division, and for this reason there would be no discomfiture at the meeting of competitors for lunch.

The situation was now nerve-racking for me. For over two years I had dropped all other business interests and concentrated total efforts on the Arabian Gulf dry dock project. If it fell through, and it was looking mighty precarious, I would have to divert my attentions to something else. Such a prospect was too horrendous to contemplate, and it strengthened my resolve to push AGRY to a positive conclusion.

Back in London I received a cable from Dr. Taher saying it was OK to approach Vickers. I telephoned Sir Leonard Redshaw at Barrow-in-Furness and explained briefly what I wanted to talk to Vickers about. He was friendly and gruff as always, and invited me up to Barrow, reminding me that I knew the way. I travelled by train, changing at Crewe. Archie White met me at the station and drove me to the yard. It was as though a flashback to 20 years previously – Len Redshaw, Bill Richardson, Archie White and I sitting in the room overlooking the yard, with its cranes and slipways and a lot of activity in the naval section, two cargo vessels and a ferry boat on the merchant side. It was no longer possible to tour the yard because more than half of it was a restricted area because of Royal Navy work.

I outlined AGRY's history; after listening to the exposé, Len said it might be interesting, and as Vickers had such a large workforce (over 6,000), if incentives were there, he could spare 170 technicians from divisional managers, etc., down to foreman level. Because they operated and part-owned the Masagon dock yard in India, and also managed the Karachi repair yard, they would be able to recruit skilled and unskilled labour from a reliable source. (It sounded marvellous!) Vickers also had no objection to co-operating with KHI, although Vickers saw no problem doing the whole job themselves. Len said the decision could not be taken by himself alone, and wanted me to meet Peter Matthews, the Managing Director of the whole Vickers Group, of which the shipbuilding division was only a part. Len said that Peter would be away until the end of the month, but he would let me have an answer as soon as possible. On arriving back in London I found a cable from Dr. Taher from San Francisco advising of his arrival in London the following Saturday. I telephoned the Taher boys' school and spoke to the headmaster, telling him that the boys' father was arriving on Saturday. I asked if the boys could take the train to London on Sunday morning, saying I would see that they got back to school in the afternoon. Whilst chatting about the boys, he disclosed that they were very devout, and when prayer time came during the day, they would disappear into the lavatory to pray. However, after the first week, Khalid had told his brother this was wrong and now when it was time to pray, they did so openly before the school. Apparently, the other boys respected this and did not tease them. The head confirmed the boys would be on the train arriving in London around 10:00 on Sunday. Sheikh Yamani and Dr. Taher are both deeply religious, and it was evident that Dr. Taher had brought up his sons sharing his religious devotion. When Dr. Taher and I met on Saturday night, I told him of the remarks from the headmaster about his sons having changed their place of prayer. He was very proud of Khalid and Tarik for their courage amongst strangers. He thought the Vickers news was hopeful so far as it went.

The next day we collected the boys at the station and drove out to Prince's Club – a sports' club for boys – so that Dr. Taher could see their proficiency at waterski-ing. We lunched and afterwards drove down to the school. Dr. Taher wanted to see the school and to meet the headmaster as he would possibly send the boys back the next year.

On Monday Dr. Taher flew back to the Kingdom. There was now a different set of pieces to the puzzle. We still had SENER and KHI, but if we got Vickers, would they approve the SENER lay-out, as Len Redshaw was a very authoritative person and would want to do it his way? Vickers was studying the copy of the SENER design. The cash flow calculations were bound to alter, at least on the hull side, and would have to be re-worked with Vickers' input. It was an impatient ten–day wait until I would hear from Len Redshaw. He telephoned me on Friday, 30 July, and on behalf of Peter Matthews invited me to lunch at Vickers House the following Monday. I was shown up to Peter Matthews' office. In his early 40s he seemed a young man to hold such an important position in established British industry. He was tall, angular and muscular, and looked like a cricketer. Len Redshaw was also present. The room was large, overlooking the Thames, and at one end a table had been set for lunch. After a pink gin (the naval drink), we sat down at the table and immedi-ately began to talk about AGRY. Len had briefed Peter Matthews, who fired a number of pertinent questions at me. He was amused at the possibility of co-operating with KHI, a company with which they were normally in fierce competition in the sale of helicopters, aircraft compo-nents, marine engines, and even printing presses, as both companies manufactured similar products in their various divisions. He said he had not met any of the KHI management as his company had extensive dealings with another Japanese giant (the name of which was discreetly withheld). At the end of the meal, Peter Matthews said that at this time he could indicate no more of Vickers' interest than that he had authori-zed Len's division to study the project. He said Len would be in touch with me for any information required. We said goodbye and Len stayed behind while a secretary showed me to the lift.

At a second meeting two weeks later Peter Matthews advised me that, subsequent to tying up a lot of loose ends, the project interested Vickers. He said Len would like to talk to someone from KHI about the apportion-ment of responsibilities and requested me to arrange for KHI to send a representative familiar with AGRY to Barrow-in-Furness. I telephoned Toshio Kawakami and told him about Vickers, and their possible interest. I asked whether he and Mr. Ishige would fly to England and meet with Len Redshaw in Barrow for discussion on AGRY. By his reaction I could tell that, somehow, I had transgressed the code of etiquette in this matter. He said he would telephone me later. He did so in about an hour, and suggested that I come to Tokyo with someone from Vickers. Peter Matthews' reaction was 'Oh God, typical Japanese stickiness.' He asked me to try and get KHI to England, as Len Redshaw could not get away from Barrow before the end of the year as he was completing a large naval competitive bid and they had two launches of vessels at which he had to be present. I promised to do what I could, even if it meant going to Tokyo to persuade KHI to come to Barrow.

In Tokyo, I mentioned that Dr. Taher hoped a meeting could take place between KHI and Vickers this year, so that the matter could be reported at the OAPEC meeting scheduled for mid-November. Dr. Yoshida said he would be happy to oblige Dr. Taher, and that it would be possible for Mr. Kawakami and Mr. Ishige to arrive in London on Sunday, 31 October, prepared to meet with Vickers. I flew back to London the next morning.

An uninvolved reader will probably find the 'toing and froing' set out in such detail both boring and unnecessary. I would like to assure that reader of the necessity of all the travel and discussion. Whereas the dry dock was of some importance to OAPEC when they thought of it as the first Pan-Arabic non-oil-related industrial project (I have already explained why I found it personally important), to the giant old established industries we were trying to attract as partners to the venture, it was relatively insignificant in terms of revenue, or even public relations. My job was to keep them excited by the project, especially of the possible spin-off of being associated with the rich, emerging Arab world, but I could not hold out any hope of oil being part of the equation. The personal meetings kept up the impression of movement, and many more hints could be divulged than would have been possible in a letter or telex. A meeting enabled the involvement of many more witnesses (especially in Japan) than the telephone could. Each time one appeared with a bulging briefcase, the parties to the meeting hoped it contained some, as yet, undisclosed 'goodies'.

On Sunday, 31 October Toshio Kawakami and Mr. Hosocki (head of KHI's London Office) came to dinner at home. They both felt the Vickers inclusion in the management structure would be of great benefit to AGRY. Mr. Kawakami was in general agreement with the figures prepared by Len Redshaw. He also felt that their experience on the Indian continent in operating dry docks would be a reliable source of skilled and unskilled labour, rather than having to depend on a labour contractor and obtaining unknowns.

Peter Matthews welcomed Messrs. Kawakami and Hosocki the next day. Archie White was present, as both Len Redshaw and Bill Richardson were occupied in Barrow at the ceremony of launching a Royal Naval frigate. This meeting was not intended to be a working session, but merely for KHI to inform Vickers of their interest in co-operating with them. Mr. Kawakami wanted to agree a convenient date with Mr. Matthews for a formal meeting between the two companies, for which Dr. Yoshida would fly to London. Thursday, 18 November was agreed. On that date Vickers would arrange a lunch for Dr. Yoshida, Messrs. Kawakami, Redshaw, Richardson and myself. A ritual was taking place, in which all performers had to follow the script. After lunch the KHI representatives returned to Tokyo.

Nothing much happened until I heard from Peter Matthews that, in principle, Vickers were interested to progress further. On 16 November

Peter Matthews and Len Redshaw dined with me at home to consider a programme to be pursued after the formal meeting with KHI on 18 November. I was very keen to get Vickers and KHI together in the Arabian Gulf to inspect both sites, make a recommendation of their choice, get the revised design costed, get new cash flow projections, and put the whole package together with a draft management contract before OAPEC for their consideration. We all agreed to push forward in that direction before OAPEC cooled off after so many changes of shipyards – UCS, Swan Hunter, AESA/KHI, and now Vickers/KHI.

Lunch on 18 November was a success, and both companies declared their interest in proceeding. The following day Dr. Yoshida, Mr. Kawakami, Mr. Ishige and I went to Barrow by Vickers' plane and returned that evening. Mr. Kawakami and Mr. Ishige remained behind in Barrow to work on details with the Vickers team of experts. Both Vickers and KHI were getting along well, and gave me some cash flow projections which were slightly more encouraging than the previous ones.

Dr. Taher and I met in Jeddah on Saturday. I gave him the new forecasts and was able to tell him that it had been agreed Vickers would go to Tokyo early in the New Year (1972), and then both Vickers and KHI would visit the Gulf and make their recommendation about the siting of the dry dock. Dr. Taher said I was not to make a report for the forthcoming OAPEC Conference, but to defer it until the March meeting, when something definite could be put before the Committee.

I returned to London and met with Mr. Kawakami, who was on his way back to Tokyo. He said that the four days of meetings in Barrow had been very fruitful and nothing more could be done until the Arabian Gulf visit in the New Year. After telephone calls to Len Redshaw and Bill Richardson it seemed that they also felt satisfied with progress and now looked forward to site examination in the Arabian Gulf.

It was mid-December and Marcella and I decided to drive down to Florence to spend Christmas with Marcella's mother. It was all very enjoyable and far removed from AGRY. We arrived back in London in time to spend New Year's Eve of 1971 at Annabel's.

# 9

# JANUARY – APRIL 1972

It was now January 1972. 1971 had, in many ways, seemed like a diplomatic mission. There was always a formality in dealing with Sheikh Yamani, a Minister of his King, who was addressed as 'Your Excellency', as were the OAPEC Ministers, but KHI and Vickers required by far the most delicate handling. Perhaps it was because they were both such old companies that the etiquette of yesteryear still clung.

On 4 January 1972, I had a meeting with Peter Matthews at his request. He informed me that Sir Leonard Redshaw and Mr. Richardson were flying to Tokyo on 15 February to meet with KHI and then proceed together to the Arabian Gulf. I said I would advise Dr. Taher.

I flew to Switzerland to meet Dr. Taher, who was in Geneva working with an OPEC Committee. He thought that the dry dock matter should be presented to OAPEC for their consideration at the March meeting, and asked me to keep pushing everyone forward, as it would be the end of the project if anyone were to drop out at that point. On arriving back in London there was a meeting with Len Redshaw, at which he gave me a bound study which had resulted from the combined work of KHI and Vickers. There were two copies – one for Dr. Taher.

On 22 January I flew again to Geneva, this time to meet Sheikh Yamani, who was attending an OPEC meeting there. Sheikh Yamani said he had heard from Dr. Taher that there seemed progress, and he was pleased such first-class companies as Vickers and KHI were interested in the management of the dry dock. I gave him my copy of the Vickers/KHI preliminary feasibility study. He said Dr. Taher would probably be in London in February and could possibly meet with Vickers before their departure to Japan.

When I arrived back in London, the evening news reported that the OPEC meeting had broken up in disarray, and Sheikh Yamani had walked out. OPEC contained Iranian, Venezuelan, Nigerian and Indonesian members, whereas OAPEC was solidly Arab. I felt pleased it was not before OPEC that the dry dock project would be heard. In the world of the Gulf Arabs, King Faisal was the most exalted person, being protector of the Holy Shrines of Mecca and Medina. In temporal matters, no man on the Arabian Peninsular was more respected than Sheikh Yamani. His counsel and opinion carried great weight, and all the Gulf States were aligned with his policy.

At the end of January there was a further meeting with Len Redshaw, who had obtained the wage scales of the required Pakistani skilled and unskilled workers, and Vickers had now been able to arrive at an accurate wage bill for AGRY. I told him I had learned Dr. Taher would be in London in February and would like a meeting with Vickers. Len said that he had to be in Washington, but Bill Richardson would be happy to come down from Barrow to meet Dr. Taher.

On 10 February Bill Richardson and I had breakfast with Dr. Taher at the London Hilton. Dr. Taher took an immediate liking to Bill, as anyone would. He has an expansive personality and a contagious sense of humour. Dr. Taher said he hoped this trip would see the end of the troubles that had inhibited the dry dock project getting off the ground. Bill Richardson spoke reassuringly about how well Vickers' management had worked with Pakistani and Indian labour, and volunteered that for a dry dock in the Arabian Gulf, it was a better solution than a 100 per cent British workforce, in view of the climatic conditions. Dr. Taher said he looked forward to meeting again in the Kingdom. (Bill was surprised by this remark, thinking the Kingdom of Heaven had been meant.) Dr. Taher had another visitor announced and we departed. Bill went to purchase some up-to-date Admiralty Charts of the Gulf, which was called 'Persian' by everyone except those dealing with the Arab states bordering it.

I flew to Tokyo on 14 February in order to get there a day earlier and make sure everything had been organized for the arrival of Len and Bill. Of course, I need not have bothered, as KHI efficiency had planned every moment from meeting them at the steps of the aircraft, taking care of their passports and baggage checks, and driving them straight to the New Otani. Passports and baggage were delivered to their rooms half an hour later. As a courtesy, Len and Bill were left on their own the rest of the day to recover from possible jet-lag. They were told a car would collect them at 9:00 the next morning to transport them to the KHI office.

On Thursday Mr. Hasegawa, Dr. Yoshida and Mr. Kawakami formally received Redshaw and Richardson. After a few gracious words from both sides, we adjourned to the room with the long table. Again on one side were Mr. Hasegawa, Dr. Yoshida and Mr. Kawakami, with a further twelve young unidentified Japanese scribes – translators, engineers and architects. On the other side were Len, with Bill and myself on either side of him. It was surprising, but there was almost no disagreement on the management structure, or general operation of AGRY. Len Redshaw, however, felt strongly that the site of AGRY should be Bahrain, subject to physical investigation of the load-bearing substructure. He pointed out that ship-repairing involved a lot of coming and going of people who might not be able to obtain a Saudi Arabian visa in time, and their non-admittance could delay the ship. He also said the prohibition of alcohol in Saudi Arabia would be a deterrent to ships crews' acceptance of AGRY. He was worried that this would provoke unpleasant incidents where drink would be smuggled in and ships' crew, or even yard workers, caught by the Saudi Police. As there were neither immigration nor alcohol difficulties in Bahrain, he felt it would facilitate the operation of AGRY. KHI felt as he did, and both asked if I could approach the subject with Dr. Taher, as they did not wish to appear critical of Saudi Arabia.

We all lunched in the Chinese restaurant on the top floor and then, as a special homage to Vickers, we were driven to the shrine of the 'Makassar', the battleship built in Barrow by Vickers in 1900. It is a national monument and rests in a concrete dock at Yokosuka, near Yokohama.

That evening we were entertained by KHI at their guest house and ate a traditional Japanese ceremonial dinner (the same one with the many courses given by Mitsubishi for Dr. Taher). The following day had been reserved by KHI for visits to their two main shipyards at Kobe, and the brand new one at Sakaide. We made an early start, taking the very fast, streamlined, 150 mph bullet train to Osaka, then a car to Kobe. The Kobe yard was similar to Barrow in that they built naval and merchant vessels. It was old, big, and employed many workers. We had dinner at another KHI guest house, where a geisha girl sang traditional airs to a tune picked out on a one-string guitar. Afterwards, Bill Richardson asked if he could try to play the instrument, and gave a very good rendition of 'Oh, Suzannah'. By then the party got very merry and the innocuous saki flowed. It was such a convivial drink that no one had taken whisky or gin, both of which were offered.

The next morning a large KHI-built helicopter picked us up; we flew low over the Kobe yard to get an aerial view, proceeding cross country to Takamatsu, where the Sakaide shipyard is located. It incorporated the latest innovations of modern shipyard technology. It had two vast dry docks and mammoth cranes. Large sections of the VLCC were prefabricated in a huge, high roofed, shed. The roof would slide back, enabling the crane to transfer the 800 tons of worked steel into the dry dock, where it was welded to the partially assembled VLCC. Mr. Hasegawa was very pleased to show Vickers the method they had devised of automatically welding both sides of a seam by applying the machine to only one side of the steel plate. Probably nowhere else at that time could a VLCC be built so rapidly. They completed four a year in each of the dry docks.

After lunch the helicopter flew us to Tokyo Airport, where Len

Redshaw, Bill Richardson, Toshio Kawakami, Mr. Ishige and I boarded a Pan Am flight to Karachi, from where we changed aircraft and continued to Bahrain. We checked into the Dilman Hotel, as the new Gulf Hotel was not yet complete. Archie White had arrived from England and greeted us.

We dined together and had an early night as a Bahrain Government car was collecting us at 8:00 to take us to the Ministry of Development & Industry to meet the Minister, Yousuf Al-Shirawi. We did not know it then, but Yousuf was to become very much involved in the dry dock project. He was a tall man, always dressed in Western clothes, even in the Arab world. He looked more like a Levantine than an Arab. In fact, except for being very much taller, he strongly resembled the Greek ship-owner Aristotle Onassis. His charm, vitality, and sense of humour, were also similar. He was Bahrain's Minister on the OAPEC Council of Ministers. We were shown into his office and he welcomed Len Redshaw, Bill Richardson, Archie White, Toshio Kawakami and Mr. Ishige. Yousuf and I had met previously at OAPEC meetings in Kuwait, Algiers and elsewhere. He was a great promoter of Bahrain and had been responsible for most, if not all, its recent development. Under him a large aluminium smelter had been built with the Swiss firm of Alusuisse, using Bahrain's natural gas as fuel. He was very hopeful that the dry dock would be situated in Bahrain, and had asked the Port Captain to take us out in the government launch to visit two sites, both of which might be suitable. He reminded us that Bahrain had evolved from a British protectorate – in fact, he called himself an Anglo-Bedouin. He pointed out the ease with which we had entered Bahrain, even without a visa – a visa for four days was issued on the spot. He also mentioned there were no restrictions on drink.

A car took us into the port, which used to be the British Royal Naval Station, HMS Juffair. There was a long pier, at which a number of ships were tied, including the yacht of the Ruler of Bahrain. Capt. Duck led us to the launch, which we boarded. It was a mild, sunny day. We looked at the two sites, both of which seemed suitable, subject to in-depth study. They had access to the deep water channel, large ship anchorage, and turning basin. We thanked Capt. Duck for his time, returned to shore, checked out of the Dilman and were driven to the airport, where we took a flight to Dhahran. Although we were met by a Petromin representative, it was still necessary to pass the usual immigration and customs formalities. Customs opened all our bags, and when searching Archie's suitcase, found a bottle of 'hair tonic'. The official unscrewed the cap, smelled the contents, said, 'Whisky,' and smashed the bottle on the floor. It was only after a long conversation between the Petromin representative and the customs man that Archie was allowed into the country. I never knew whether Archie had actually tried to smuggle in a drink, or whether it was on Len's instruction to test and see how seriously Saudi Arabia controlled the import of alcohol. In either case, he found out.

1. The Amir Of Bahrain, H.H. Sheikh Isa Bin Sulman Al Khalifa, on his right
H.E. Sheikh Ahmed Zaki Yamani and other dignitaries at the Inauguration Ceremony,
15 December 1977

2. Sir Julian Hodge and the Rt. Hon. George Thomas, Speaker of the House of Commons, at the Al Hada Palace as house guests of H.E. Sheikh Ahmed Zaki Yamani on the occasion of a party given for H.M. King Khalid, Summer 1977

3. The two Marcellas, Princess Marcella Borghese on the right and Marcella Rossi on the left as house guests at the Al Hada Palace, Summer 1976

4. Gifford S. Rossi during his war service years 1939–1945 – Eagle Squadron

5. Gifford S. Rossi delivering his speech at the Rotary Meeting in Bahrain,
1 December 1974

6. Gifford S. Rossi photographing the progress of the work on site

7. The first ASRY Agents' Meeting in Bahrain, 23 June 1977

8. Gifford S. Rossi's working chair and desk, two of the most treasured pieces of his French Empire Collection

9. Marcella Rossi arriving at the Kandarah Palace *en route* to Al Hada, Summer 1976

10. H.E. Sheik Ahmed Zaki Yamani at one of the many OAPEC Meetings attended by Gifford S. Rossi

11. Marcella Rossi looking at the dock plan in the Hyundai Office, 30 November 1974

12. H.E. Mr. Yousuf Al-Shirawi at one of the many OAPEC Meetings attended by Gifford S. Rossi

13. Gifford S. Rossi and H.E. Sheikh Ahmed Zaki Yamani

14.  Gifford S. Rossi signing the Management Contract in Cairo, 11 July 1974

15.  The Amir of Bahrain, H.H. Sheikh Isa Bin Sulman Al Khalifa at the Inauguration Ceremony in Bahrain; the Cartier Gold and Silver model of the  shipyard is in the foreground, 15 December1977

16. The Amir of Bahrain, H.H. Sheikh Isa Bin Sulman Al Khalifa, H.E. Sheikh Ahmed Zaki Yamani and H.E. Mr. Yousuf Al-Shirawi arriving at the Inauguration Ceremony, 15 December 1977

17. H.E. Dr. Abdulhady H. Taher and his sons Tarik and Khalid at the Prince's Club, Summer 1971

18. Gifford S. Rossi and H.E. Mr. Majid Al-Jishi hosting the lunch given for the ASRY Agents in Bahrain, June 1977

19. Gifford S. Rossi and H.E. Mr. Majid Al-Jishi on their own at the ASRY Agents' lunch in Bahrain, June 1977

20. Gifford S. Rossi in the 'hard hat' area on site, June 1977

21. Gifford S. Rossi sitting in front of the full length portrait of Napoleon by Gérard, 1970

22.  Gifford S. Rossi at home in his study, 1972

23. H.E. Mr. Yousuf Al-Shirawi and Gifford S. Rossi – meeting at home in the study

24. Gifford S. Rossi on the day of the
Inauguration Ceremony,
15 December 1977

25. Marcella Rossi getting ready for the
Cornerstone Laying Ceremony,
30 November 1974

6. Gifford S. Rossi between geisha girls at a dinner hosted by Kawasaki Heavy Industries in Tokyo, September 1972

27. H.E. Dr. Abdulhady H.Taher and Gifford S. Rossi – lunch at the Beau Rivage in Geneva – talks on the dry dock project, April 1973

28. Photograph of the dry dock, February 1975

29. Photograph of the dry dock, January 1976

30. Photograph of the dry dock, July 1976

31. Photograph of the dry dock, January 1978

**STATE OF BAHRAIN**
OFFICE OF THE PRIME MINISTER

دَوْلَـةُ البَحَـرَيْنِ
رِئاسَةُ بِحَـلِسِ الوُزَراءِ

30th November, 1974

Dear Mr. Rossi,

        The occasion of the Dry Dock Project
Ceremony provides me with an opportunity to thank you
for all your assistance in bringing the Dry Dock concept
to this stage.  Although there have been many factors
which have contributed to the Dry Dock achievement, I
know that your vision, optimism and energy have been
amongst the most significant.  You have always been
willing to travel and to meet those concerned with
the project, at any time and in any place, and it is
this personal involvement which has been so important
to keeping the project moving.

        We all know that although the Dry Dock
Project has come a long way, there is yet further to go,
and it will need more of your perseverance and energy
to help complete the Project.  I look forward to your
continuing help, which I know the Project needs, so
that we may together bring it to successful completion.


        Yours sincerely,

KHALIFA BIN SULMAN AL-KHALIFA.



Gifford S. Rossi, Esq.,

32.  Letter from the Office of the Prime Minister, State of Bahrain, H.E. Sheikh Khalifa
Bin Sulman Al-Khalifa, 30 November 1974

33. Marcella Rossi on a pause to Al Hada during Ramadan, Summer 1976

34. The band '*style Anglais*' on the day of the Inauguration Ceremony,
15 December 1977

35. The Amir of Bahrain, H.H. Sheikh Isa Bin Sulman Al Khalifa, and dignitaries looking at the dry dock on the plan on the day of the Inauguration Ceremony, 15 December 1977

36. Jack Hartshorn, 1969          37. Don Fernando de Azqueta, 1971

38. A quick stop in France in the Porsche on the way to Bilbao, 1971

39. Marcella Rossi arriving in Madrid, 1970

40. Gifford S. Rossi – one more waiting lounge in the 1970s

41. Gifford S. Rossi on a short break in Cairo on the way back to London, 1974

42. Marcella and Gifford S. Rossi in front of the *Mobil Pride* docked for the Inauguration Ceremony, 15 December 1977

We all checked into the Al-Khobar Palace. That evening after dinner, Len chaired a meeting of Bill Richardson, Archie White, Toshio Kawakami, Moto Ishige and myself. He said that in order to consider objectively the AGRY project, they would view the Dammam site and then be able to report to Dr. Taher, who was meeting us the next day. He asked if I had cleared the matters raised in Tokyo with Dr. Taher. I said I had done so before the Tokyo trip. Dr. Taher's view, and most importantly, Sheikh Yamani's, was that the dry dock was an OAPEC project, and it must be located in whichever OAPEC country provided the optimum conditions. Petromin was the project leader, but did not expect preference to be given to Saudi Arabia. I explained I had not mentioned this in Tokyo because I did not want everyone to assume the site would be Bahrain before taking a further look at Dammam Pier, which Vickers had never visited. Vickers and KHI felt much more optimistic about the project after their visit to Bahrain, which had an indigenous population of 300,000, many of whom were second generation graduates of British schools. It also had the highest concentration of local industry of any of the OAPEC countries at that time, even to the extent of having two successful small (up to 4,000 tons) shiprepair yards operating, one of them run by the British Company, Gray Mackenzie.

Early the next morning, KHI and Vickers made a conscientious inspection of the Dammam Pier site. While there, we learned of extensive expansion plans which had been approved and would make it impossible to accommodate the dry dock. Therefore, as it transpired, like it or not, Dammam was ruled out.

We were received by Dr. Taher in the offices of Petmark, where we had a working lunch. Dr. Taher advised us that the development of the Dammam Pier area would provoke the siting of the dry dock in Bahrain. His eyes twinkled as he said probably neither Vickers nor KHI would object. He asked if any decisions about management had been reached. Len Redshaw said that Vickers would be happy to associate with KHI in the management of the OAPEC dry dock, and both companies believed that Bahrain was a suitable location which offered a good site in deep water. Dr. Taher said, 'Good,' and turned to me and asked me to prepare a report to that effect for the next OAPEC meeting on 4 March, about ten days hence. He said that if OAPEC approved the proposal, the respective lawyers of Vickers, KHI and OAPEC should be alerted in order to draft a Management Contract. We said goodbye to Dr. Taher and were hastily driven to the hotel for our bags, then out to the airport, where we caught a Saudi Airlines domestic flight for Jeddah. We were in time to catch the British Airways flight (BOAC) to London via Beirut. Our Japanese friends left the flight at Beirut and headed east with another airline.

We landed in London on the morning of 24 February. This left me five days to prepare the OAPEC report, which I wanted to take with me and deliver personally in Kuwait to the secretariat on 1 March to make sure it would be included on the Agenda of the meeting under 'Any Other Business'. In Kuwait I did some lobbying for the dry dock project in the two remaining days until the meeting, but this time I felt confident we had the right team, and that the project would be approved at the OAPEC Ministerial Meeting.

The meeting lasted two days with a long Agenda, the dry dock coming last. On 5 March, OAPEC approved proceeding with the dry dock, managed by Vickers and KHI, to be located in Bahrain. This was a jubilant moment at the end of three years' uphill slogging. The next day Souheil Sadawi asked me to draft a Letter of Intent to be signed by him and sent to Vickers and KHI. Suddenly there seemed nothing to do except sit in on discussions with lawyers, who had started drafting the Management Contract. On Thursday, 23 March, Peter Matthews' secretary telephoned me to ask if it would be convenient for me to come to Vickers House the following day. I accepted, expecting that he wished to discuss a point in the Management Contract. When I arrived, I found Archie White was already there. After I was seated, Peter Matthews came directly to the point by saying that Vickers had tendered for three submarines for the Israeli Navy. The outcome of the competition would not be known until 25 April, when the bids would be opened. He realized that if Vickers were awarded the submarine contract, they would have to withdraw from the OAPEC project, and would probably become blacklisted in the Arab world. He felt it was correct to alert me, in the event of the submarines being awarded to Vickers. I told him the act of tendering would not break the link with OAPEC, but if Vickers were to build the submarines, clearly OAPEC could not accept them as managers. Peter Matthews said Vickers recognized this, but they had an obligation to the large workforce at Barrow, and they had to go after all business which would employ them. He said that Vickers had no political views in the Middle East, and they would be reluctant to withdraw from the OAPEC project. Therefore, if I could generate for Vickers work of equivalent man hours to the three submarines, whether in the form of frigate, through deck cruiser, early warning defence system, or any other hardware produced at Barrow, Vickers would back away from the submarines for Israel. I said that, of course, I would have to report the matter to Dr. Taher and Yousuf Al-Shirawi and perhaps, with luck, alternative work could be found for Vickers.

I wondered whether AGRY could survive the blow, because a number of OAPEC states, jealous that Bahrain was nominated as the dry dock site, would openly voice their view that the whole matter had gone on too long, and if Vickers had to withdraw, why not drop the whole project instead of having to search again for new managers.

On 28 March I went to Barrow to try and learn from Len Redshaw how good Vickers believed their chances were of being awarded the submarines. Len answered honestly that these were quite good because one of the standard submarines Vickers built was particularly suited to the type of work Israel had in mind. This would not be welcome news in the Arab world. I flew next day to Kuwait to meet with Souheil Sadawi, who was furious at the news and wanted to blacklist Vickers at once. I explained that through the Foreign Office, with whom I had met, meetings were being arranged with the Ministry of Defence to determine if a Royal Naval order could be accelerated, which would give Vickers equivalent work to the submarines, and other avenues were being explored as well. If we succeeded, and Vickers dropped the submarines, this would be a blow to Israel. Souheil Sadawi liked that. I nevertheless asked his authority quietly to start looking for a substitute for Vickers if they had to withdraw. He authorized this.

I then flew to Bahrain to inform Yousuf Al-Shirawi. He was very disappointed and, together, we called on the British Ambassador to explain the matter. He had already been informed by the Foreign Office of the 'regrettable situation', and hoped a solution would be found so that Vickers could fulfil their management function. We then went to Government House, where his Highness the Ruler, the Prime Minister and the Foreign Minister were in session. Yousuf asked me to explain the Vickers position. I added that I had obtained permission from the OAPEC Secretary General, Souheil Sadawi, to search for yet another shipyard, in case it became necessary to dispense with Vickers. The Prime Minister asked me to start looking at once. Yousuf suggested I try to persuade KHI to assume the full management role. I agreed to do both, and left for London.

On Wednesday, 5 April, I met with the Middle East Desk at the Foreign Office, who were doubtful about being able to provide alternative work to enable Vickers to drop the submarines. The following Friday I saw Peter Matthews to tell him that I must start looking for another yard on a conditional basis, in the event Vickers would have to withdraw. I was able to tell him officially that OAPEC would ask for Vicker's resignation from the dry dock project if they contracted for the Israeli submarines. We both agreed it would be a 'damned shame'. I had telephoned Toshio Kawakami about the possibility of Vickers winning a bid for three Israeli submarines as soon as I had heard about it. He flew to London and we dined together that evening. I told him about my meeting with Peter Matthews, which had taken place that afternoon. I then told him that Yousuf Al-Shirawi had asked me to sound out KHI about taking on the full management role. Toshio Kawakami said it was impossible for the reasons which had been explained many times. He asked what I would do, and I said, 'Pray that Vickers' bid is turned down by the

Israelis.' Toshio Kawakami stayed on in London for another week in case there were any developments which required him.

There was only one last hope for a management partner – Lisnave. It was the one I had been avoiding because of its Chairman's statement to the press about not wanting to create a competitor. Lisnave was the world's only purpose-built VLCC repair yard, now with three dry docks, enjoying a tremendous boom, with shipowners paying premiums for a position in the queue to be dry docked, due to the world shortage of VLCC dry docks. Although AGRY could become a competitor, it was no longer a case of Lisnave establishing it. This had been done by OAPEC approving the project and announcing the location as Bahrain. It was now a question of Lisnave possibly joining with its competition, rather than fighting it. AGRY had received considerable press attention over the past year, and it seemed that Mr. de Mello, the Chairman of Lisnave, must accept that AGRY would be built, especially with the wealth of OAPEC behind it. Thus fortified in my thinking, I flew to Lisbon on Sunday and stayed at the Hotel Ritz (owned by de Mello interests). On Monday morning I telephoned the Lisnave office and spoke to Manuel Perestrello, the Managing Director, whom I had met several times at Chamber of Shipping dinners in London. I told him I wanted to talk about AGRY, and a possible role for Lisnave. He laughed and said, 'We were waiting for you.'

Manuel de Mello was by far Portugal's largest industrialist, and probably its wealthiest citizen. His grandfather had been brought back to Portugal from exile following a revolution 60 years earlier, which preceded Salazar's long dictatorship. The first de Mello brought about the industrialization and commercialization of Europe's most backward country. Apart from Lisnave, de Mello interests owned the CUF Group, which comprised more than 100 enterprises, including the Imperio Insurance Company, shipping companies, banks, hotels, department stores, etc. He was also the father of 12 children.

A secretary showed me into the sumptuous office, where Mr. de Mello shook hands with a firm athletic grip. He was of medium height, powerfully built, sun-tanned, his dark hair greying, about forty-five, and spoke unaccented English. He sat silently while I told my story, which ended with an invitation to join KHI in the management of the OAPEC dry dock, which would be built in Bahrain. He asked about Vickers. I said I believed they would be awarded the Israeli submarines, and that even if they were not, their position *vis-à–vis* the OAPEC principals must become difficult, as some states felt it was an unfriendly act just bidding for the submarines. He smiled, held out his hand, and said, 'I will talk this over with Mr. Perestrello and telephone you in a few days.'

I returned to London. The following day, Wednesday, Len Redshaw and Bill Richardson came to lunch. Len said that Vickers felt it would be correct at this time to sever ties with the OAPEC project as it now seemed almost certain that they would be awarded the contract for the submarines. Peter Matthews had advised Mr. Hasegawa of KHI accordingly. It was a sad ending to what had appeared such a prestigious solution for the management of AGRY.

The next day Mr. Kawakami and I met and I told him about Lisnave. He, of course, knew Lisnave as KHI had two turbine experts at Lisnave on a six-monthly rota basis. He was not optimistic about them being interested in managing AGRY, as they had such a heavy programme of their own, with more ships to dock than they could handle. As KHI were unwilling to assume the management role alone, I asked Toshio Kawakami if he could suggest some other suitable shipyard we could recruit. He said he didn't know of any as at that moment all VLCC yards were very busy with their own production.

On Friday morning, 14 April, Mr. Souheil Sadawi telephoned to say he was at the London Hilton and would like to speak with me. I fixed a time for that afternoon and went to see him. He told me, it seemed with some pleasure, that OAPEC wished me to ask Vickers to withdraw from the project. I replied that the previous day I had sent letters to him and Dr. Taher to report that Vickers had advised me that as the submarine order seemed probable, and as a substitute employment of their labour force had not been found, with reluctance, Vickers much resign from the OAPEC dry dock management. Mr. Sadawi seemed relieved and said, 'What are you going to do now? In three years you haven't found managers, surely you don't believe you will be able to find some acceptable yard.' He told me the feeling amongst the OAPEC members was that the project should be abandoned. I knew I would get a hostile reception if I were to speak of Lisnave, which in any case had not yet indicated their interest, so I replied that I still believed very much in the validity of the project, and that each passing month increased the requirement for an Arabian Gulf dry dock. As consultant to Petromin I must take my instructions from them, and as yet they had not told me to abandon the project. The meeting over, I left, realizing that pretty soon I would have to pull a rabbit out of a hat, or OAPEC would drop the dry dock project. Even Sheikh Yamani and Dr. Taher could not keep OAPEC enthusiastic without some positive progress.

On Sunday night Yousuf Al-Shirawi telephoned to tell me he was in London and suggested I come and have a meal with him. By contrast with the discussion with Mr. Sadawi on the previous Friday, Yousuf, in his ebullient manner, blew the breath of life again into the dry dock scheme, which Bahrain wanted, even as a commercial project, and which they would finance if OAPEC got cold feet. I pointed out to Yousuf that the dry dock could never be commercially viable as the investment could not be amortized, even without interest, over 20 years. I then told him about

Lisnave being a possibility, but no more than that. I reported that KHI had again turned down the complete management role for the same reasons previously given. Yousuf then asked me about Lisnave – if it was impressive, and if Portugal looked like a wealthy country, or like the Third World, which he said most of OAPEC probably thought it was. I told him Lisnave was the most impressive ship repair yard in Europe, it was brand new, that Lisbon looked very prosperous, and that the Ritz Hotel looked better and cleaner than the old Ritz in London. Yousuf then said, 'If Lisnave are interested, here is the policy we will follow. Get them to invite the Secretary General of OAPEC to visit the yard.' Yousuf said that Souheil Sadawi would certainly accept the invitation to see the shipyard, and as this was bound to create a good impression, he would give his support of the project within OAPEC, which it lacked at the moment.

I felt considerably cheered after my meeting with Yousuf, but of course, everything depended on Lisnave being interested.

# 10

# APRIL – SEPTEMBER 1972

On Tuesday, 18 April, Mr. de Mello's secretary telephoned to ask if I could come to Lisbon for a discussion with Lisnave the following Friday. I flew to Lisbon on Thursday, 20 April and again stayed at the Ritz. At 10:00 the next morning a car came to take me to Lisnave, about a 30–minute drive across the imposing Salazar bridge, and then along the south bank of the river to Almada, where the huge cranes of the shipyard loomed above the surrounding fence. I had seen many photographs of Lisnave, but had never seen the yard, which was made more impressive by the high hulls of empty VLCCs waiting to dock. There were three in dock and nine others tied up, either waiting to dock or being worked on alongside. All the famous funnel markings were there – Esso, Shell, Texaco, Livanos, Onassis, Bergeson, Salen. There were probably five million DWTs of crude oil carriers in the shipyard.

I met the Managing Director, Manuel Perestrello, the Deputy Managing Director, Nils Eckerbom (a Swede), and the New Projects Manager, Antonio Caetano Carreira. They asked me to tell them about AGRY. After about half an hour's patient listening, I had finished giving them all the pertinent facts. They asked whether it would be necessary to share the management with KHI if Lisnave became interested. I said OAPEC would feel morally committed to KHI as they had expended a great deal of work, time and money on the project so far. Lisnave said they had no objection to working with KHI, and mentioned the two KHI turbine specialists permanently at Lisnave in case special problems arose on Japanese turbines and gears. Manuel Perestrello said, in principle, Lisnave was interested, but they had a lot of ground to make up. They wanted to meet with KHI and visit the site. I suggested that perhaps it would be helpful in progressing matters if they could invite the Secretary General of OAPEC to visit Lisnave, so that he could tell the Ministerial Conference that he had seen the yard and met its top executives. I said I would be going to Kuwait shortly, and would be happy to deliver the invitation. Manuel Perestrello called his secretary in, got the correct spelling of Mr.

Sadawi's name and dictated the letter of invitation, which he gave to me before I left in the afternoon.

In the mean time, I was taken on a comprehensive tour of Lisnave, followed by lunch in the executive dining-room, in which Mr. de Mello had placed some of his large collection of English silver. I was then driven back to the hotel to pick up my bag and taken to the airport to catch the evening flight to London.

I sent a full report to Dr. Taher and Yousuf Al-Shirawi the next day, and prepared a further report to send to Kuwait for the secretariat to distribute to the OAPEC meeting scheduled for 6 May. On the night of 3 May I was at the Kuwait Sheraton. The next morning I walked over to the nearby OAPEC headquarters and was received by Souheil Sadawi. He had been given a copy of my report and had read it. I gave him the glossy, illustrated brochure of Lisnave which, in its way, was a work of art. I showed him the *Financial Times* article of two years previously, in which Mr. de Mello, when asked about his interest in the management of the OAPEC dry dock, had said he was not about to establish competition for Lisnave. I pointed out that it was quite an achievement for OAPEC to have gained world credibility for its intention to build a dry dock in the Arabian Gulf. Proof of this was that Lisnave now recognized the dry dock would be built, and were probably willing to participate in its management after a detailed study of the project. I then gave him Manuel Perestrello's invitation to visit Lisnave. He visibly began to change his mind, and to say why not a Portuguese shipyard, especially such a famous one. I believed the OAPEC meeting might agree to continue with the investigation of the dry dock project.

On the day before the OAPEC Conference, I had a meeting with Sheikh Yamani, Dr. Taher and Yousuf Al-Shirawi, brought them completely up to date, and gave them each a Lisnave brochure. They already knew of Mr. Sadawi's invitation to visit Lisnave. Sheikh Yamani said that his and Dr. Taher's confidence in the merit of the dry dock continued, and he would try to persuade the OAPEC Conference not to discard the opportunity of creating a VLCC dry dock in the Arabian Gulf.

The following day the OAPEC Conference authorized further investigation of the dry dock, with Lisnave, and voted that the Secretary General accept the invitation to visit Lisnave and form his own impression about its suitability as eventual managers. Yousuf Al-Shirawi's plan had worked.

Back in London the following day, I sent memoranda concerning the OAPEC meeting to KHI and Lisnave. On Thursday, 11 May, I flew to Lisbon and overnighted at the Ritz. The next day I went to Lisnave to deliver copies of the most recent studies, drawings and other data on AGRY, to serve as background to their own investigations. I advised them that Souheil Sadawi would arrive in Lisbon on Sunday evening, 14 May, and that I had reserved a suite for him at the Ritz. I explained that I had to return to London that day, but would be back on Sunday to accompany Mr. Sadawi to the shipyard on Monday morning. Manuel Perestrello said a car would collect us at 10:00 and after a short talk with top management Mr. Sadawi would be taken on a tour of the shipyard and go on board a VLCC, which would be followed by lunch.

On Sunday I was back in Lisbon to meet Souheil Sadawi at the airport, where he arrived from Beirut. Lisnave had arranged VIP treatment. A car drove me to the steps of the aircraft to pick him up, he surrendered his passport and baggage checks, and we were driven straight to the Ritz. His suite at the Ritz was a good deal more lavish than the London Hilton, and had its own large balcony, with flowering shrubs, overlooking Lisbon. It was warm enough to have a drink outdoors, and we sat on the balcony until the bags and passport were brought up to his room.

Lisbon is an undeniably beautiful city, verdant with exotic foliage and the blue blossoms of the jacaranda tree were evident on several long avenues visible from the hotel. Mr. Sadawi was hungry and asked if I knew a good restaurant. I asked if he preferred fish or meat – he said he liked fish, so we went to Gambrinus, one of Europe's best fish restaurants. He had grown quite fond of Portugal by the time we got back to the hotel.

The following day the visit to Lisnave went very well. Souheil had never seen a shipyard, or a VLCC. The first time aboard a VLCC is an impressive experience, the sheer size and height of the vessel astonishes. When I took him to the airport that evening, he remarked, 'Well, I hope Lisnave won't withdraw from the project because they seem very good.' I stayed in Lisbon a further day in order to meet with Caetano Carreira, who had gone through the previous projections worked out on AGRY revenue. He felt they wanted to start from scratch and make new forecasts based on Lisnave's actual experience in repairing VLCCs. He intended to show actual costs versus estimated ones, as neither AESA, Vickers nor KHI had repaired a VLCC. This made sense and was a welcome suggestion.

Back in London I lunched with my old friend, Jack Hartshorn. He was interested in the long successions of ups and downs which we had experienced, and we both agreed it would not have gone this far without Sheikh Yamani's support. Jack said he believed there would soon be an increase in oil prices, which should make OAPEC countries more inclined to invest in AGRY.

Lisnave telephoned to ask me to come over for further discussions on Thursday, 25 May. Mr. Carreira presented the new cash flow summaries and it was gratifying to see that they were slightly more positive than the old ones. On the other hand, Lisnave did not agree with the SENER layout. They said that within the de Mello Group of companies they had their own civil engineering firm, Profabril, which had designed and supervised the construction of Lisnave. Profabril were now designing a second de Mello yard in Setubal (to the south) with docks for both building and repairing VLCCs. As Profabril had a great deal of experience in VLCC yards, it was suggested the AGRY project would benefit from their assistance. This made sense, but I also recognized it as a ploy for work to be awarded to another de Mello company. This would cause considerable embarrassment with SENER, who had been in the project from the beginning, and had done an enormous amount of work. I said I would refer the matter to Dr. Taher.

On my return to London that evening, there was a message to telephone Yousuf Al-Shirawi at the Hotel Churchill. We met the next day and he told me that Bahrain, for its own account, had engaged the British firm of civil engineers, Sir Alexander Gibb & Partners, who had done a great deal of work in Bahrain. Gibb would study the two sites in Bahrain, sink some piles, and determine whether the bottom structure was sufficiently load bearing. He had asked a partner of Gibb to join us for lunch. This was the first occasion I met John Corney, with whom so much work on AGRY was done. John Corney said the two selected sites might be operationally suitable, but he was very concerned that they would not be able to support the weight of a dry dock filled with water plus a VLCC.

There had been a lot of movement since I last met with Toshio Kawakami back in April, and although he had been kept informed by telephone and memoranda, it seemed that in order to avoid misunderstandings, or that dreadful 'loss of face', I should meet with him and Dr. Yoshida. On 10 June I flew to Tokyo and on arrival Sunday morning was again met by the KHI car and taken to the New Otani. A 9:00 Monday morning, the car collected and took me to the World Trade Centre Building, where I met with Dr. Yoshida, Mr. Hasegawa and Mr. Kawakami. I told them that Lisnave had indicated interest in the AGRY project, but of course, before taking the matter further, OAPEC would like to know if KHI would join in the Management Contract on the same basis as had been contemplated with both AESA and Vickers. I gave KHI the revised cash flow projections which had been done by Lisnave. Dr. Yoshida said he had heard Lisnave expertise praised by the Japanese Sanko Steamship Company, which had docked several of their VLCCs there. Dr. Yoshida told me to thank OAPEC for their consideration in first finding out KHI's opinion before making a commitment with Lisnave. Dr. Yoshida said that KHI would be pleased to work with such speciality VLCC repairers as Lisnave, and he saw no conflict of interest. He believed the combination would be good for the AGRY project, and that soon he and Mr. Kawakami would come to Europe personally to meet with Lisnave. We lunched together and I flew back to London. The one-day turn arounds on the eleven-hour flight between London and Tokyo were very tiring and I began to feel that Agry was causing me to log too many flying hours.

Much of the feeling of adventure may seem to be lost as the reader follows, or loses track of, the repetitive itinerary between London, Arabian Gulf and Japan. However, I found plenty of drama as the plot unfolded. In reality, a lot was being asked from the necessary managers who, if eventually identified as being responsible for AGRY, would be risking their international reputation amongst ship-owners if AGRY was unable to carry out satisfactory shiprepairs. A delicate balance was needed in gauging their remuneration in the way of a management fee – enough to lure them, but not too much so as to reflect negatively on AGRY's cash flow. That was the easy part, as one was dealing with experienced professionals who knew what it was all about. On the other hand, the principals – OAPEC – knew very little about ship-repairing, or its need, often being blinded by the technical matters involved, and yet querying matters which had previously been explained and agreed. Really, they could not say why they were pursuing a dry dock in the Arabian Gulf – in all probability the reason was because Sheikh Yamani believed in the project. All of the changes in the selection of managers, and even the selection of site, tended to unnerve them. Frequently, they had to be re-motivated by positive news, done mostly by providing international newspaper comment praising OAPEC on its foresight in causing AGRY to be built, and then going on to say how much such a facility would be used. However, all of this tended to collapse when it had to be pointed out that AGRY would not be a commercial venture.

On 20 June there was a formal meeting at home between Dr. Yoshida, Messrs. Kawakami, Perestrello and Carreira, at which both parties agreed to co-operate. This was followed by dinner at the Royal Thames Yacht Club, which was also attended by Yousuf Al-Shirawi. Yousuf asked me to draw up a Letter of Intent for both KHI and Lisnave to sign. Dr. Yoshida and Mr. Kawakami flew back to Lisbon with Perestrello and Carreira, but all agreed to return to London on 29 June.

In the mean time, a Letter of Intent was drawn up, which I would endeavour to get Dr. Taher to approve and sign. Dr. Taher was in Geneva because of an OPEC Conference, and a short meeting was arranged, during which he signed the Letter of Intent. On 29 June, Dr. Yoshida and Manuel Perestrello signed the document on behalf of their companies. It committed all three parties to pursue the project, at least up to the point of providing a firm proposal on which OAPEC could decide.

As a pleasant diversion, Khalid and Tarik Taher arrived at the beginning of July. In a year both had matured and were fluent in English. Earlier in the year, Dr. Taher had asked me to find a place more academically advanced where the boys could study other subjects in their school curriculum besides learning to speak English. Places had been found for them at Bournemouth College, which ran an international summer school. We all had dinner together at home, after which they returned to their 'home from home' at No. 11 Cadogan Gardens. The boys became so fond of No. 11 that they persuaded their father to forsake the big hotels and try it. He liked it, but required better telephone communication, with a dial telephone in his room, rather than having to go through a switchboard. We drove the boys to Bournemouth to register and be shown their accommodation as classes started the following day.

On Monday, 3 July Marcella and I were in Zurich to attend the wedding of my 83-year-old uncle. He married a Swiss nurse. In July 1989 he celebrated his 100th birthday, so the marriage and nursing must have both proved healthy.

The following Thursday Dr. Taher and I had dinner. He observed that it seemed we were getting closer to realizing the dry dock. I had become very cautious and agreed we had a potential management team lined up, but I expected we would find some engineering problems, and told him that Yousuf had engaged Sir Alexander Gibb & Partners to make a mechanical investigation of the two proposed sites. It was disclosed that the design suggestions of Profabril differed from SENER, which I felt would lead to abandoning our old friends, SENER. Dr. Taher acknowledged that this was unfortunate and thought it would be a good idea to go to Spain and talk with them, possibly asking them to submit their fee for work carried out to date. Sheikh Yamani and Dr. Taher were always conscious of obligations, and keen to observe business ethics. This was very much King Faisal's policy, which gave Saudi Arabia a reputation for reliability and many transactions were initiated and continued without a written contract. Perhaps this was due to the fact that it was bewildering to consider which court could have jurisdiction as the law of Saudi Arabia was Shari'a, the Muslim code of religious law. Later in the 1970s, more and more contracts did specify that British Law applied.

I did not look forward to my meeting with SENER, as it is never a pleasant thing to bring bad news to a friend. As it happened, SENER dealt with the matter with the utmost good will and said they had anticipated this when AESA dropped out, and if Vickers had stayed, they would probably have wished to nominate their own construction engineers. As soon as they had learned of Lisnave's involvement, it was assumed Profabril would become the chosen engineers. I said that Bahrain had engaged Sir Alexander Gibb & Partners to do some preliminary site investigation. We lunched together and I conveyed Dr. Taher's appreciation of the help that SENER had given. Some months later, SENER submitted a modest account for their fees, which Petromin paid immediately.

John Corney of Sir Alexander Gibb submitted the preliminary site survey, which I circulated with a covering letter to Sheikh Yamani, Dr. Taher, Yousuf Al-Shirawi and Souheil Sadawi. Although Gibb were working for Bahrain, as it was on the OAPEC dry dock, everything was channelled through me for redistribution. The report was not encouraging about the two sites originally chosen, mainly due to insufficient load bearing. Gibb recommended reclaiming sand and aggregate from the sea bottom by the use of large dredgers, compacting this, and forming an island on which the dry dock/repair yard would be located. The dry dock would be excavated from this artificial island, which would be situated in deep water and connected to the mainland by a causeway. The report suggested that this innovative scheme would be less costly than sinking hundreds of steel piles to support either of the other two sites.

Marcella and I decided it was time to take a holiday and left by car for Greece. Some Greek friends had developed a new hotel, with bungalows on an unspoilt virgin shore, with a central restaurant for meals, except breakfast, which was brought to the bungalow. It was on the Island of Evia. It had been built by a wealthy man and the bungalows were so luxuriously outfitted that after two years he realized it was not a good business proposition and sold it to Club Méditerranée, which commercialized it. We were lucky to be there during its first year of operation. No telephone had yet been installed, and one shipowner who was staying received communications from his office by daily helicopter. We thoroughly enjoyed the break, and were back in London before the end of August.

On 26 August Khalid and Tarik came to London as the school term had finished. We dined together at home and learned that Bournemouth College had been much more serious than their previous school. Both Khalid and Tarik had been taught some advanced algebra, which Khalid told us was a discipline invented by an Arab scholar in the ninth century. The next day we put them on a flight to Jeddah and told them we hoped to see them the following summer.

I telephoned Manuel Perestrello and learned that he had arranged with Mr. Kawakami to come to Tokyo on 2 September, and from there a joint KHI/Lisnave visit to Bahrain was planned. He suggested we meet in Lisbon to discuss the programme, in which it was assumed I would join. I flew on the Thursday and we went over the programme, which appeared well planned. Mr. Perestrello introduced me to Jao Cabral, the Managing Director of Profabril, who showed me the proposed layout for AGRY. It was a different concept from the SENER one and comprised a number of steel workshops and other equipment as support facilities for the dry dock. I was insufficiently technical to comment, but Mr. Perestrello was of the opinion that, from AGRY's viewpoint, it was a very practical layout, with a uniflow system of movement within the repair yard. It clearly envisaged the full-fledged repairs Lisnave undertook, rather than the simple docking previously intended to clean hull, remove marine growth, repaint hull, pull tailshaft out and inspect sea valves, etc., mainly aimed at maintaining vessel speed. AGRY had now been planned as the latest word in the way of a sophisticated VLCC repair yard, incorporating a dry dock. It would be even a slight improvement on Lisnave, but with only one dock. No costing had yet been estimated, pending the site visit. Mr. Cabral was planning to join us when we arrived in Bahrain. I was able to return to London the same day.

The next morning, Friday, the day before my departure to Japan, I met John Corney at the Gibb office and told him about the Profabril yard layout. I persuaded him to meet us in Bahrain, so that in discussions with Yousuf Al-Shirawi, John Corney's comments could be heard in relation to the Profabril scheme. Our schedule put us in Bahrain on Sunday, 10 September, and John Corney agreed to be there on that date. Manuel Perestrello, Fernando Alves (Lisnave's Commercial Director), and Antonio Caetano Carreira met me at London Airport and we all took the flight to Tokyo over Anchorage. This flight took an hour longer than via Moscow, but the equipment used, the Boeing 747, was more comfortable than the DC8 or 707 used on the Moscow run. We were the only passengers in the front of the aircraft and had the upstairs lounge to ourselves. All the way to Anchorage we discussed every aspect of AGRY, including Lisnave's ideas about the amount the management fee should be. At Anchorage there was a vast, stuffed, polar bear, whose pelt was kept a snowy white, although it had been looming there on its hind legs for a very long time in the fogs that invaded the lounge three months of the year. At Tokyo Airport we were expected and driven to the Imperial Hotel, this at the request of Mr. Perestrello who always stayed there when visiting Lisnave's Japanese agent (who provided 50 per cent of Lisnave's business). I was quite happy to stay at the Imperial again, and it made it easier for cars to collect us all from the same hotel. We were left alone after arrival on Sunday. It was raining, so a walk was not inviting. Instead we went for a swim – I find exercise after a long flight helps to fight jet-lag. I still believed in the recuperative Japanese massage – equally as good at the Imperial as at the Okura – after which I slept soundly. We all met up in the lobby at 9:00 for two KHI cars to take us to the World Trade Centre Building. Dr. Yoshida, Mr. Hasegawa, Mr. Nomura (an Executive Vice-President), and Mr. Kawakami welcomed Lisnave most cordially.

We proceeded to the familiar room with the long table, where KHI seated themselves on one side, and the Lisnave three and I sat opposite. So much of the ground was familiar to KHI that it came as a surprise when Caetano Carreira produced the new layout of AGRY, prepared by Profabril. It included complete machinery shops for dealing with turbine repairs, turning of tailshafts, balancing and repairing of propellers, even gears could be serviced. There was an electronics shop. Mr. Carreira pointed out that this was more essential in the Arabian Gulf than in Japan or Europe, where there was a back-up from the engineering industry. If a ship came into AGRY in trouble, and not just for cleaning and painting, AGRY had to provide the repairs required, or it would soon be labelled by the industry as inadequate. A sensible argument which KHI saw, but new studies and calculations would have to be made, and the Japanese input of engineers would be substantially increased.

It was agreed that as soon as the site visit had been made, both companies would co-operate on a feasibility study in depth, costing the yard construction, its operating overheads and its revenue. This document would be aimed at becoming the definitive basis on which OAPEC would reach its decision to proceed with AGRY or not. I asked when such a study could be completed. Both sides believed it would be ready during the first half of October. Lisnave would furnish the building cost of AGRY in conjunction with Profabril, as well as man-power costs, excluding KHI technicians. Estimates of revenue would also be provided by Lisnave based on actual docking and repair bills of Lisnave. It was agreed that AGRY's prices must be competitive, therefore it was realistic to use Lisnave's revenue estimates.

There was a further day of meetings at which the format of the feasibility study was finally agreed by all parties. We boarded the aircraft on Saturday morning to fly Tokyo/Hong Kong/Bombay/Bahrain, where we arrived during the early hours of Sunday, 10 September. We were all accommodated at the Gulf Hotel, which had been completed.

On Monday morning we spent more than two hours with Yousuf Al-Shirawi in his office at Government House. John Corney and Jao Cabral had arrived the previous day. Also present was Majid Al-Jishi, Yousuf's deputy, a qualified engineer able to discuss marine construction matters in Bahrain. The meeting comprised a complete exposé of AGRY, presented by Caetano Carreira and Toshio Kawakami. Yousuf was concerned by the increased cost which the more comprehensive equipping of AGRY would provoke, but he accepted the argument that to operate as an acceptable shipyard it had to provide all the services a shipowner needed. AGRY had to be self-reliant, as big pieces of a ship's machinery could not be sent by air to Europe or Japan for repair. Mr. Perestrello described some of the major items of repair which Lisnave had encountered on VLCCs. Yousuf accepted the logic and said he hoped that OAPEC could find the money.

The next day we all visited the site with Majid Al-Jishi. John Corney explained very concisely why the creation of an artificial island in an advantageous location in deep water seemed the optimum solution. Jao Cabral agreed. It was evident there was no conflict of interest between Gibb and Profabril.

On Saturday, 16 September, Yousuf arranged for us all to pay our respects to His Highness Sheikh Isa the Ruler. We assembled and took seats in the throne room of the palace. We were served Arabic cardamom coffee in small cups, which kept being refilled from a large, long spouted, brass vessel. Toshio Kawakami remarked to the Ruler how green Bahrain was, with its palm trees and grass. His Highness replied that God had given them water wells, but he was sorry that God had forgotten the oil wells. We all laughed. The audience was over. That night Yousuf gave a large party which included the British and Swiss management of ALBA (Aluminium Bahrain). ALBA was one of Yousuf's promotions for Bahrain and it had become a successful large aluminium ingot producer.

On Sunday, 17 September, we all dispersed east and west to commence work on the feasibility study, which we hoped would be the document on which OAPEC decided to proceed.

# 11

# SEPTEMBER 1972 – JUNE 1973

On 19 September, Sheikh Yamani made a speech in London in which he outlined his proposals for 'Participation' in which the oil producers would share more equitably in the control of their own oil production with the concessionaries who heretofore had paid royalties and taxes only to the owners of the oil wells.

My involvement in the nuts and bolts of AGRY began with the massive paperwork which the feasibility study generated. KHI and Lisnave supplied the input, with all the numbers agreed between them, but as English was not their native language, they enlisted me to edit the text of the 196–page report. A great deal of the work was merely translating from fractured English to a more fluent version. It was like going to an engineering school for me, and, assuredly, KHI and Lisnave were good professors. They explained all the information which was contained on each page. My own contribution was on the marketing side, determining the size of the market, and how AGRY could go about capturing its share. The report projected a build-up from 32 ships per year, to a throughput of 50 ships annually in the third year.

I remained in Lisbon from 25 September until 7 October, working with Ishige and Kawakami and seven Lisnave specialists assigned to the study. On 7 October Kawakami, Ishige and I transported to London 50 numbered, printed copies, in large canvas bags. We had selected green hardback covers for the report, with lettering in gold. The green was the same colour as the Saudi Arabian flag, which uses the colour of the banner carried by the camel troup of Abdul Aziz ibn Saud when he led his small corps into the Hejaz, uniting the tribes to form the Kingdom of Saudi Arabia. We had developed a romantic attraction to AGRY, and were prepared to carry the concept of the Arabian Gulf Repair Yard into battle with its detractors.

On the Friday before completing the report, we had a meeting with Jose Manuel de Mello who had been through the draft feasibility study which he considered a factual and accurate presentation of the project. The document estimated the cost of building AGRY at $146 million. On

Monday numbered copies were airfreighted to Sheikh Yamani, Dr. Taher, Yousuf Al-Shirawi, and Souheil Sadawi, as well as 25 copies to the OAPEC secretariat. For two weeks there was no reaction, not even a meeting with KHI or Lisnave.

On Sunday, 22 October, I telephoned Bahrain and spoke with Yousuf to ask whether a date had been fixed for an OAPEC meeting which would consider the feasibility study. He said the next OAPEC meeting would be in Kuwait on 18 November, but he would like to see me before that date, and suggested I came down to Bahrain. I flew out on 26 October, and as the next day was Friday, I lunched with John Green, the British manager of BASREC (Bahrain Ship Repair and Engineering Company), owned by one of Bahrain's most important merchant families, the Kanoos. It was a most enlightening discussion. John Green, a professional shipbuilder from the Tyne, had been in Bahrain for about seven years. Although BASREC was a small yard concentrating on the repair of tugs, dredgers and service vessels, it had done well financially and carried out some sophisticated repairs on large ships which had suffered breakdowns. It had no dry-dock. He thought AGRY would be inundated with business, as more and more large tankers were coming to the area, and most of them to the Aramco terminal at Ras Tanura, about 30 miles away. He said AGRY must not assume that all vessels would be gas free, and that it should definitely include a tank cleaning station, pointing out that no such facility existed in the Gulf and therefore it would be a useful complement to AGRY. He was very helpful and recognized there was no conflict of interest between BASREC and AGRY.

The next morning I went to Government House and had a long meeting with Yousuf and Majid. Majid thought the feasibility study was a thorough exposition of the dry dock project, but felt that the findings would disappoint the OAPEC members who were expected to invest in it. He asked whether, between KHI, Lisnave and myself, a way could be found to increase the profitability, and even to make it a commercial proposition with the initial large investment recovered over a 20-year period. He said he was aware we had always said it was not possible to make the dry dock commercially viable, and accepted that the high construction cost of $146 million, compared with $40 million for Lisnave which had three dry docks, made this difficult. Yousuf was dubious of OAPEC's reaction, as they would not be investing in their own countries, but spending their money in a fellow member's country – Bahrain. To stimulate their enthusiasm for such investment, he said we must find a way to provide them with an acceptable return on their stake. This was bad news indeed, as I could still see no way of turning AGRY into a commercial proposition. It was explained again that most shipyards throughout the world required subsidies from their governments, which were given because the industry was such a large employer of workmen, who would otherwise have to be supported by national assistance at a greater cost to the government involved. I told Yousuf I would go back to Lisnave and see what we might be able to invent.

On Wednesday, 1 November, I flew to Lisbon and spent three days there going over the problem of investment return raised by Bahrain. We re-examined the repair revenue estimates, which were based on a realistic progression from simple maintenance dockings, building up to expensive sophisticated repairs, and tried to accelerate the progression. Even erring on the side of optimism, this only made a modest improvement in profit forecasts, and far too little to enable repayment of the initial investment over 20 years, even without interest. I reverted to the argument developed a couple of years previously – if 1 US cent per barrel of oil lifted from the OAPEC states was added as an incremental loading charge allocated to the OAPEC dry dock fund, this would permit repayment of total investment over 10 years, plus interest, as 1 US cent on 7 million barrels per day would generate over $25 million per year. With the general trend of rising oil prices, this seemed a modest increase – oil at that time was about $3 per barrel.

When I arrived back in London, I prepared a memorandum outlining the proposal for creating additional income for AGRY, albeit unearned. When it was ready, I decided to send it exclusively to Yousuf because Sheikh Yamani and Dr. Taher had never voiced any concern about AGRY not being commercially viable. In their view, it would be considered a national project and a technical training facility, providing practical engineering experience.

Yousuf unexpectedly arrived in London before my memorandum, which I had sent to Bahrain, reached him. He telephoned and invited me to lunch the following day. So preoccupied was he that OAPEC would not find the dry dock project an interesting investment, that he had flown over to learn what progress we were making towards improving the dry dock cash flow. I had brought a copy of the memorandum, which he read, thought for some minutes, and said it would not work as it was not equitable. The dry dock was to be financed by OAPEC, with each member state including Bahrain, putting up an equal share of its cost. My proposal put the brunt of the financing on Saudi Arabia, which was the largest oil producer in OAPEC, followed by Kuwait. Together, their 1 US cent per barrel would account for 75 per cent of the funds allocated to the dry dock. What was worse, Bahrain would not be contributing anything of consequence, as it exported next to no oil. He said that he, as Bahrain representative on the OAPEC Ministerial Council, would be embarrassed by such a proposal if it was put before OAPEC.

I told him with regret that neither Lisnave, KHI nor I could find any other solution. The best realistic result we could forecast for the dry dock was that it would pay its way and not require any annual subsidy, apart from the grant to cover its building cost. Yousuf was disappointed. He told me to come to Kuwait for the OAPEC meeting, as all the Ministers would have received their copies of the feasibility study, and no doubt have the comments and advice of their British and American consultants. He expected that I would be asked a lot of questions and he hoped I would get in some positive lobbying.

On the way to Kuwait I stopped in Beirut to see Maurice Brunel, who was in charge of Petromin's office there. We had not met for some time and not since the site of the dry dock had been moved to Bahrain. I learned from Maurice of the almost impossible administrative problem, at least from Saudi Arabia's situation, of diverting revenue from the Ministry of Petroleum to an OAPEC fund. Saudi Arabia's investment in the OAPEC dry dock would be derived from a quite different route. He was not pessimistic about the outcome of the OAPEC Conference, because he believed Sheikh Yamani was behind the project and no OAPEC member had the stature or sufficient knowledge of what was good for the region, to oppose him.

I arrived at the Kuwait Sheraton too late to see anyone on the Friday evening (17th), but I was up early on the morning of the meeting. I saw a few of the Ministers walking about, or talking amongst themselves. Several were holding the rather thick, green-covered, feasibility study. None of them, or their foreign advisors, approached me, and it would have been impossible to go up to them and ask how they liked the dry dock project. The meeting lasted two days, of which most discussion dealt with the price of oil. At the finish of the meeting, I saw Sheikh Yamani briefly. He said OAPEC were unable to decide. They were still interested in the project, but felt the feasibility study was theoretical and should include a market survey reporting on meetings with ship-owners and their views about using the dry dock, possibly even obtaining some letters of intent about their willingness to use it.

Sheikh Yamani flew back to the Kingdom and I had a meeting with Yousuf about how to proceed. I knew that it was an Arab tendency not to turn propositions down, but rather to delay decisions and postpone a rejection. It seemed that this process was commencing, and I asked Yousuf his view. He said it wasn't as bad as that, but Ministers were reluctant to go to their governments and recommend an investment in the $150 million dry dock construction cost, which a feasibility study had clearly shown would not be recovered. I mentioned to Yousuf my fear that KHI and Lisnave, who were very busy in their respective shipyards, might themselves lose interest in the project, to which both had devoted a good deal of unpaid time and out-of-pocket expenses. I asked Yousuf whether he could arrange for an OAPEC Committee of perhaps himself and Dr. Taher to come to a meeting at Lisnave, which would be attended by KHI, and we could openly discuss the dry dock project, its aims, its revenue possibilities, and OAPEC's attitude. Yousuf said he could organize it from the OAPEC side if I could set it up in Portugal.

I left Kuwait with a quest, which always made me feel more optimistic. I returned to London on Monday, 20 November. On Tuesday I flew to Lisbon to report on the indecisive OAPEC meeting. I asked whether Lisnave would be prepared to host an AGRY meeting, with KHI present, attended by Yousuf Al-Shirawi and Dr. Taher, who would represent OAPEC. It would be an open forum for discussion of the dry dock project and there would be an opportunity for Lisnave and KHI to ask the OAPEC representatives their intentions. Manuel Perestrello said this was a good idea and Lisnave would be pleased to act as host. After a few telephone calls to Japan and Bahrain (which had a telephone link to Saudi Arabia), a date was found mutually acceptable, the meeting being scheduled for 6–7 December. Dr. Yoshida, Mr. Hasegawa and Toshio Kawakami would come from Tokyo, Yousuf Al-Shirawi would attend, but Dr. Taher was unable to come as he would be in America. He was sending in his place Mr. Jamal Jawa, the Deputy Governor of Petromin.

Unfortunately, on 30 November, I came down with a severe case of 'flu, with a high fever. It persisted, and on 4 December I was still in bed and had a temperature of 39°C. It was too late to postpone the meeting, and as I had no intention of missing it, on 5 December Marcella and I flew to Lisbon. My doctor gave me an injection, which reduced the temperature, and I was taking antibiotics. Nevertheless, I boarded the aircraft as a walking case of pneumonia. We went to our room at the Ritz and I got straight into bed, hoping to feel better for the meeting the following day. The next day I had no fever, which I took as a good omen, but I was still coughing badly.

On 6 December at 9:00 we all met in Lisnave's lecture hall. The meeting commenced by Caetano Carreira showing slides of the lay-out of AGRY, photographs of the body of water from which the island would be reclaimed, sketches of the engineering steps involved, and then a schedule of construction costs was shown. The presentation went on for about an hour; we then moved to the Boardroom and found seats around a U-shaped table. (I learned later that I had given Yousuf my germ as I sat next to him at the meeting table.) We talked long and hard about the project. We got nowhere because it was impossible to generate enough revenue from repairing 50 ships per year at competitive prices, to pay back the approximate $150 million investment.

Mr. de Mello joined us at lunch, after which the meeting continued until 17:00. It was again inconclusive, as there was no way of achieving what the OAPEC delegates wanted. Both Yousuf and Mr. Jamal Jawa accepted this, but they did what I had hoped they would, which was to declare OAPEC's continuing strong interest in the construction of a dry dock-repair complex in Bahrain. The point which emerged from the meeting was that OAPEC would like KHI, Lisnave and myself to make an intensive market survey, and, if possible, to visit those ship-owners which had the majority of VLCCs. KHI made Toshio Kawakami available, and Lisnave appointed Fernando Alves, the Commercial Manager, both of whom would accompany me to the US, England, Greece and Norway. These visits were to take place early in the New Year. As the meeting had no further business to discuss, it broke up without continuing into the following day.

Jose Manuel de Mello had planned a reception and dinner for us in his château outside Lisbon. I had to decline because by then I was pretty sick and headed for bed at the Ritz. A local doctor, and Marcella, looked after me for five days until I was fit to return to London. I said my goodbyes to Yousuf and the others over the telephone before their departures.

It had been a good exercise in public relations. The appearance at Lisnave of Yousuf and Jamal Jawa had gone a long way to convince KHI and Lisnave that OAPEC were not losing interest in the project, and the OAPEC delegates saw, for the first time, a really large, efficient, modern VLCC repair yard, similar to what the OAPEC dry dock would resemble. They also recognized that the OAPEC dry dock had a pair of very competent managers. It could be reliably reported to the OAPEC Ministerial Council that all of the right components were there to make a success of the dry dock.

We got back to London on 12 December and I began to plan an itinerary for our visits to the shipowners in four countries. New Year's Eve was on a Sunday so there was no Annabel's. 1972 ended with some progress having been logged during the year, but I had a premonition that there was still a long way to go.

On 3 January 1973 I had a long meeting with Peter Fisher, the Editor of Lloyd's List, who had received so many enquiries about AGRY from shipowners that he wanted to feature AGRY as a front page editorial, giving all known information about the OAPEC dry dock and when it was expected to become operational.

Peter Fisher's article appeared and it was a good one. He avoided mentioning that OAPEC had not yet approved it, merely stating that OAPEC had accepted the management team of Lisnave and KHI, and the siting of the dry dock in Bahrain. He predicted that the dry dock would be able to receive its first ship in 1977 (four years hence). This went a long way to establish AGRY in the minds of shipowners as a reality. Lloyd's List is every week day's compulsory morning reading by shipowners and their staff. On the other hand, we were not making fast progress towards OAPEC actually agreeing to fund the project, and were still searching for a way to make it commercially viable. Our marketing trip was to commence in New York on 15 January. On the 7th I flew to

Lisbon to meet Manuel Perestrello to agree the list of visits to shipowners we would make on the east and west coasts of the US, as well as in Europe. He added a few names to the list, and it was arranged that Fernando Alves, Toshio Kawakami and I would meet on Sunday, 14 January, at my Club in New York (the Metropolitan), where we would all be staying.

On Monday, 15 January, we met two Marine Vice-Presidents of Esso and had a long discussion. They presented a number of technical arguments in support of AGRY, and said that if it became operational they would certainly use it, although it would have to be an emergency to cause them to be the first to use the facility.

It would be highly repetitive to refer to each meeting, because virtually everyone said the same thing – 'AGRY would be a great convenience.' 'They had confidence in the management, as both companies were well known to them.' 'There were too few VLCC repair yards.' 'Bahrain was an acceptable and pleasant site, with none of the problems experienced in other Gulf states.'

We visited 15 major shipping companies, both oil company and independent, on the east coast, and four on the west coast, the largest being SOCAL (Chevron) in San Francisco. In writing up the reports of the 19 meetings, it was amazing how similar they were. Not one meeting generated negative reaction to AGRY. In fact, it seemed that everyone was waiting for it. We worked hard, our question and answer sessions lasting at least an hour at each meeting. We visited New York, Philadelphia, Los Angeles and San Francisco, from where we flew back to London on Saturday, 20 January.

From January 23 to 26 the same team saw Shell and BP, as well as ten independent shipowners, and then went to Paris where we met four French VLCC operators, and finally on to Athens where, by 31 January, we had met six Greek VLCC shipowners, and returned to London.

It was agreed that I would write the report on the 41 meetings with VLCC operators, send drafts to Lisnave and KHI, have it printed in the requisite 25 copies, and circulate it through the OAPEC secretariat. With the letter from the OAPEC secretariat which acknowledged receipt of the report, it was disclosed that Souheil Sadawi was no longer Secretary General of OAPEC, and that his place was provisionally being filled by the Deputy, Mr. Abdul-Aziz Al-Turki. No reasons were given.

At about that time I began to get a great deal of statistical information from H. P. Drewry, the oil and shipping economists. One of their directors, Mike Ratcliffe, was a star at forecasting shipping demand. He was very interested in feeding AGRY into his computer models of future VLCC repair trends, and probably was the first important shipping element which took AGRY for granted in long-range planning. We met frequently and his information about vessel speeds, and how the service speed dropped away month by month after the first four months sub-sequent to a docking, provided useful ammunition for AGRY. The higher the charter rate, the greater the potential money loss due to each half-knot reduction of vessel speed. At that time owners found 12 months between dockings the optimum to maintain speed, while taking into consideration the seven days lost in docking. Unfortunately, there were not nearly enough dry docks to enable this, and the intervals between dockings were running at about 24 months.

On 19 February a meeting took place in London attended by Dr. Taher, Yousuf Al-Shirawi, Dr. Yoshida, Toshio Kawakami and Fernando Alves. The purpose was to discuss the market reception to the OAPEC dry dock. All had received copies of the market study. It was unanimously agreed that there was a strong market for AGRY. Both Lisnave and KHI were champing at the bit, and asked when OAPEC would next meet to consider the project. Yousuf Al-Shirawi said that, for the moment, OAPEC was without a Secretary General. It was expected that by April a new Secretary General would be installed, and, shortly after, an OAPEC meeting would take place to discuss, and hopefully decide on, the dry dock. Dr. Yoshida respectfully pointed out that KHI had put in more than two years' work on the project and would like to be told soon whether OAPEC would proceed, or else KHI would have to drop out. I knew that this was also the mood of Lisnave, but I was in no position to push OAPEC. Consultants can only pursue the interests of their clients. I had the feeling OAPEC was deliberately delaying a decision involving massive investment. They still needed convincing beyond what the market study showed. It was indeed a delicate balance, with the risk of OAPEC postponing a decision to the point where Lisnave and KHI would withdraw from the project. In those boom shipping times they had plenty of work in their own home yards.

On Wednesday, 21 February Dr. Taher, who was still in London, asked me to meet him. He disclosed that Sheikh Yamani and some members of OAPEC were very much in favour of proceeding with the dry dock, but Sheikh Yamani was reluctant to influence the other members into a decision about which at present they were timid. Dr. Taher said that the timing was not yet right, although the dry dock project looked very good with its choice of managers and the evident strong market support. He asked me to extend all efforts to keep the enthusiasm of Lisnave and KHI at its present level, but to delay matters without misleading them, because he was sure that in the end this would be in their best interests. He then hinted that things within the oil world might become more favourable for all the OAPEC producers, which would give courage to the cautious investors. I got the message, and very much hoped that I would be able to keep our joint managers on the string.

John Kennedy, the Petromin lawyer, and I met several times to discuss the Management Contract. The Contract presented no problem as such, but neither one of us knew all of the 'duties' for which a manager of a shiprepair yard should contract. Help on this matter came from our old collaborators, Vickers. I asked Len Redshaw, who is a very bluff, tough and honourable shipbuilder, for the list of 'duties' contained in their contract for managing the Mazagon and Karachi docks. Len, who always regretted having to withdraw from the AGRY project, kindly sent me a long list of 'duties' which shipyard managers must undertake. He did not disclose their source, whether an existing contract, or something he had invented which he considered would protect the OAPEC owners of AGRY from their managers. When John Kennedy received these, he completed a first draft, which was ready by early March.

About that time, Jack Hartshorn and I had lunch. I was not able to tell him of much progress on AGRY, apart from my continuing belief in it, which I thought was also Sheikh Yamani's view. Jack again expressed his opinion that oil prices were due to rise.

On 12 March I was in Lisbon to meet Manuel Perestrello to discuss the draft Management Contract. Copies had been sent to Lisnave and KHI the previous week. The long document, with its list of duties, some-what daunted Manuel Perestrello, who said he had sent a copy to the lawyer for the de Mello Group, Dr. Sherra Lopes, who was studying it. We went through the list of duties, but there was not much comment as it was all pretty new to Lisnave. Mr. Perestrello asked for time in which to study and discuss the document with KHI. Time was a gift to the project, especially as it wasn't OAPEC asking for it.

On my return to London I found a communication from Mr. Kawakami requesting a joint meeting in April to discuss the Management Contract with Lisnave and myself. I telephoned Dr. Taher, who suggested I try to arrange a meeting with Lisnave and KHI representatives in Geneva on 2 April, which he would be able to attend.

On the 2nd Kawakami, Carreira and I met with Dr. Taher, who asked us all to have dinner with him. At dinner he questioned us about progress with the Management Contract, to which Lisnave and KHI replied that it was in the hands of their lawyers. The advantage now was clearly Dr. Taher's, and he reminded both that there would be an OAPEC meeting on 24 April, when the dry dock project would surely be discussed. Dr. Taher then mentioned that he would be asking me to go to New York to sound out some of the ship-owners previously interviewed as to whether they would be prepared to make long-term docking commitments. He said he was still searching for income which would make the dry dock commercially viable. It was his belief that everyone worked better for a company making money and standing on its own feet, rather than depending on government help. Neither Carreira nor Kawakami wished to comment on the docking contracts, but Mr. Kawakami did ask Dr.

Taher point blank if the OAPEC dry dock project would go ahead if it could not achieve commercial viability. Dr. Taher said he believed it would.

Carreira and Kawakami flew back to Lisbon together on Monday, and I to London to prepare for my American trip. On Saturday, 7 April, Marcella and I flew to New York and stayed at the Metropolitan Club annex reserved for members and their wives. We had a huge old-fashioned room which hadn't changed much or been repainted very often since Stanford White completed the Club for J. P. Morgan in the 1880s. I was pleased to be in New York with Marcella for a change. On Sunday my uncle, looking robust and well, drove in with his wife from Morristown. He said he was riding every morning and believed he would outlive his horse – the horse was 10 and my uncle 84.

The meetings were more difficult than the previous time as the questions were twice as hypothetical. If AGRY was built, would the shipowner use it? Of course he would, as there were very few other places he could go to dock his ship, and none so conveniently located. However, when it came to making a long-term docking contract, so much would depend on AGRY's performance, and AGRY wasn't yet built. The result of the investigation could be summarized by comments such as, 'If AGRY got started, we would certainly have to consider it, and look forward to further discussion at that time.' It was not disappointing, as I recognized the exercise as a ploy of Dr. Taher to show OAPEC's continuing interest in the project and their continuing quest for viability. I knew Dr. Taher did not believe in the concept of long-term docking contracts.

I returned to London where I remained until 23 April when I flew to Kuwait. Before my departure, I telephoned Mr. Perestrello in Lisbon and Mr. Kawakami in Tokyo, to learn there were several areas of disagreement between them in the Management Contract. They both regretted I could not report to the OAPEC Conference that the Management Contract had been agreed. Again, time was on the side of OAPEC.

On arrival in Kuwait at 1:00, it was found my cholera injection was out of date by a month. As my visa was in order, I was allowed to enter the country, but had to undertake to visit the Department of Health office in the port by 8:30. A few hours later I was standing in the long line of immigrant Asian workers who were waiting for their physical examinations. Eventually I reached the medical officer, who injected what seemed a very large dose of anti-cholera serum. By 10:30 I was waiting outside the conference hall. It was not a full meeting, as a new Secretary General had not yet been appointed. However, as I waited, I began to feel feverish and generally unwell. After about an hour, I went to my room, leaving a message that if I was required, I could be reached by telephone in my room. I didn't have a thermometer, but it wasn't necessary to realize I had a high temperature which, combined with nausea, must be a reaction to the large cholera shot. I became dizzy and went to bed. Several hours later, a friend telephoned to ask if I was all right. I explained about the injection and he said he would send me some tea, which would make me feel better. Shortly afterwards a waiter arrived with a pot of tea and some cakes. The tea wasn't hot, but I poured it into the cup and drank it. The tea turned out to be neat Scotch whisky. After a while I did feel better, and went down to see how the meeting had gone. The dry dock was discussed, but only in the way of reporting the market reaction to long-term docking contracts, and that a draft Management Contract was being considered by Lisnave and KHI. As the meeting broke up early, Dr. Taher, Yousuf Al-Shirawi and I flew to Beirut, and I hoped for further instructions from both of them. However, as the next day was Friday, the holy day, I did not see either of them, and took a car to visit the immense Roman ruin at Baalbek.

On the Saturday Dr. Taher, Yousuf and I met in the Petromin office. There was no doubt of the wholehearted support of them both for the dry dock, but the problem remained of finding the right time to put it to OAPEC for approval. At the moment the size of the investment, with no hope of return, would kill it off. It became clear that neither Dr. Taher nor Yousuf wished to ask me directly to delay matters, but they were sending messages which I was invited to interpret, and as long as I felt that Sheikh Yamani, Dr. Taher and Yousuf Al-Shirawi were really keen to have the dry dock built, I would try to find ways to keep Lisnave and KHI on the boil until the appropriate time for the project presentation to OAPEC.

There was no AGRY activity in London for the next two weeks. I confirmed to KHI and Lisnave that Saudi Arabia and Bahrain remained firmly in support of the project, but they had to be patient a little while longer. It seemed to me that both were agreeable to this, especially as there was a lot of work to do on the Management Contract. On 12 May Abdul Aziz Al-Turki, the OAPEC Deputy Secretary General, was in London and we met at home. He informed me that the new Secretary General had still not been appointed. He told me there would be a full OAPEC Ministerial meeting some time in June, which he would probably chair, and that he would like the meeting to consider the dry dock project. He said the picture was not yet complete, pointing out we had managers, but no Management Contract. He said there was also vagueness on the engineering side and he would like a well-known international engineering firm to price the total dry dock complex so that OAPEC would not feel they were approving something blindly, without sufficient detail.

On 15 May Toshio Kawakami was in London to meet KHI lawyers. Mr. Perestrello joined Mr. Kawakami and myself for discussion. I informed them of the meeting with Mr. Al-Turki, and his wish to have all components of AGRY ready for consideration by OAPEC at a meeting scheduled for June. They were encouraged by this, and undertook to try and reach agreement on the outstanding points in the Management Contract. I disclosed my intention of going to Bahrain to meet Yousuf to try and advance the engineering work in order to present a more precise cost picture of AGRY.

The following evening, Toshio Kawakami invited me to Claridges to meet the President of KHI, Mr. Yotsumoto. The meeting was mainly to assure Mr. Yotsumoto of OAPEC's serious intentions, as he was beginning to have his doubts about a project that had involved his company's time, efforts and expense over a three-year period. It seemed that after explanations made in the presence of Mr. Kawakami, he understood the position and said that his company was willing to carry on with the AGRY work only until the end of the year, unless something positive occurred which would justify prolonging it.

On Sunday, 20 May, I flew to Bahrain and the next day met with Yousuf. I told him of my meeting with Abdul Aziz Al-Turki, and his wish for further engineering work to determine the cost of the dry dock more precisely; I also mentioned Mr. Yotsumoto's statement that KHI would continue to support the project only until the end of the year unless there was a decision of some sort by OAPEC. Yousuf reacted immediately and said he would write to Lisnave and KHI advising them that Bahrain would engage the further services of Sir Alexander Gibb & Partners to proceed with the engineering work required for the preparation of tender documents on which to invite contractors to quote. He said that Bahrain would also engage the services of Profabril to prepare working drawings of the dry dock/repair yard which would also enable contractors to quote on its construction. Yousuf then smiled, and in an aside, said, 'That is what you Americans call putting your money where your mouth is.' Early next morning I went to Government House to collect the letters and depart for London. As soon as I arrived back, I sent telexes to Lisnave and KHI quoting the text of Yousuf's letter.

The following Monday, 28 May, there was a meeting in Lisbon with Lisnave executives, Mr. Kawakami (who had returned from Tokyo), Mr. Cabral of Profabril, John Corney of Sir Alexander Gibb, and myself. Everything was moving forward. Profabril and Gibb started work, and Lisnave/KHI and I discussed the differences in the Management Contract, subject to the advice of each party's lawyer. Except for legal language, progress was made and very few points still niggled.

Yousuf flew over to London and a working meeting was arranged for 5 June, attended by Perestrello, Carreira, Kawakami and myself. A Letter of Intent of a more advanced and comprehensive form was signed by Lisnave/KHI and Yousuf on behalf of Bahrain, in which commitments were made to engage the services of Gibb/Profabril (as the joint engineering services became called) – it was some form of document to put before OAPEC. Lisnave and KHI had committed themselves to join in a Management Contract.

On 6 June Yousuf gave a press conference to which the financial, shipping and daily papers were invited. About 20 journalists came and Yousuf aquitted himself with expertise. The ensuing press coverage was positive and AGRY came yet nearer to becoming a reality in many readers' minds.

On 11 June it was announced that the next OAPEC Ministerial Conference would be held in Damascus, Syria, on 23 June. I hoped I would be able to get a Syrian visa as this was difficult to obtain on an American passport. I tried in London, but it was impossible to arrange in the time left before the meeting, so on Friday, 15 June Marcella and I flew to Beirut. I hoped to get a Syrian visa more quickly in Beirut with the help of the Petromin office.

# 12

# JUNE – NOVEMBER 1973

On Saturday, 16 June, I met at the Beirut Petromin office with Maurice Brunel and Majid Al-Jishi. This time I had not written a report for the OAPEC meeting, as the situation had not altered since the last one. However, I learned from Yousuf that this would be necessary so I started that morning to write out a report by hand, and each evening I typed the manuscript on a borrowed machine. On Tuesday I delivered the 28 pages to the Petromin office and they made the necessary 25 copies for the OAPEC secretariat.

On Thursday, 21 June, I met with Yousuf. I had not been able to obtain the necessary Syrian visa, although I had left my passport with the Petromin office. Even without a visa, Yousuf wanted me to come to Damascus and said we would be driving there in an Embassy car with diplomatic number plates and might not be stopped at the frontier.

The next day Dr. Taher, Yousuf Al-Shirawi, Sheikh Khalifa Al-Khalifa of the Bahrain Petroleum Directorate, and I set off in two Cadillacs from the Saudi Arabian Embassy, emblazened with crests on the door, flags on the mudguards and diplomatic number plates. Dr. Taher and Yousuf were in the front car, Sheikh Khalifa and I following close behind. The road climbed up from Beirut into a mountainous region which Sheikh Khalifa said was the much fought over Golan Heights. After a drive of about one and a half hours, we reached the Lebanese-Syrian frontier. There was immediate trouble with my passport as I had no visa. Both Dr. Taher and Yousuf had diplomatic passports and they intervened with the immigration officers. Both said I was needed at a meeting in Damascus and would be returning through the same route within the next two days. This seemed to resolve the difficulty, but the Syrian official said it was necessary to keep my passport and I could collect it on the way out. I was not keen to leave it, but didn't really have a choice, and when the two cars started off, we had a motorcycle escort all the way to the hotel in Damascus.

I checked into the hotel explaining why I was unable to produce my passport. We all arranged to meet for drinks and I went up to my room to unpack and take a shower. The hotel was comfortable but hot, as there was no air-conditioning. About an hour later the telephone rang and I was asked to go down to the lobby to sign for my passport. It had miraculously arrived at the hotel, complete with Syrian entry visa, properly stamped.

That night Dr. Taher took us to a restaurant he knew; it was outdoors in a garden with flowering vines growing down the side of a stone cliff which loomed over the garden. The mezza was vegetables, pulse, chicken, lamb and unknowns and we all drank Raki (except of course for Dr. Taher). There was a hookah water pipe with a single mouthpiece which passed around the four of us at the table. I had given up smoking years before, but what was being burned in the hookah did not taste like tobacco, or perhaps I had forgotten the taste!

The following morning we went to a conference hall where the OAPEC members assembled. Abdul Aziz Al-Turki chaired the meeting again. It lasted longer than the previous one, but at its conclusion OAPEC had authorized continuing with the dry dock investigation and had approved employing engineers to proceed to the point of preparing tender documents. This relieved Bahrain of paying the cost, which was assumed by OAPEC. Lisnave and KHI would be reassured by OAPEC having committed the first million dollars of expenditure towards realizing the dry dock.

Dr. Taher and Yousuf participated in the Ministerial dinner after the meeting. Sheikh Khalifa and I went for a walk around Damascus, trying to find the ancient part of the city. After a while we tired, it was very warm and we returned to the hotel for dinner and a cold beer – Syria is not dry, although a Muslim country. Like Bahrain, foreign governments had been in residence. It was a French protectorate for a period, and much of the austerity of Islam had been diluted.

We made an early start the next morning, helped by the same motorcycle escort, which I was surprised to see Dr. Taher rewarding with a tip. We reached the frontier, passed through without passport delays, and were back in Beirut by noon. Marcella was very pleased to see me; telephone communication between Damascus and Beirut was restricted to official traffic and we had not been in touch for two days.

On Monday, 25 June, Marcella and I flew back to London. I sent identical telexes to Lisnave and KHI, reporting the outcome of the meeting. I relied for years on the use of a telex in the office of a good friend. I was reluctant to have one installed in my study at home, but realized I would have to acquire one the following year, as telex traffic between London/Lisbon/Tokyo/Bahrain/Riyadh/Kuwait was becoming voluminous.

Jack Hartshorn and I lunched on 28 June and I told him of the first OAPEC investment. He said it had been mentioned in the Middle East Economic Survey (MEES).

On Sunday, 1 July, I was in Lisbon, where the following day I met with John Corney and Mr. Cabral of Gibb/Profabril. They had jointly produced a great deal of engineering work, drawings and calculations. It was expected that the documents to accompany the invitations to tender would be ready before the end of July. They recommended a list of 20 international construction firms which should be invited to tender. The list included British, Dutch, Italian, Lebanese, French, German, Korean and Japanese companies.

In London I continued to monitor the shipping market, not only trying to assess VLCC docking demand, but trying to keep informed of any new intended VLCC repair yards being planned. Shipping and its associated components comprise a small world where nothing can be kept secret. Classification Societies, oil companies, the four or five shipping and petroleum economics firms in London, are always sources of news. Very little is treated as privileged information as, perhaps, in the financial community. It seemed that AGRY was leading as far as new dry docks were concerned, with others planned well behind, mostly owing to financing difficulties. New dry docks anywhere would have great problems to recover their investment in construction cost. The demand curve was holding, and even rising. We had not been wasting time on a useless facility. On the other hand, I was very much aware of a continuing wish on the part of OAPEC to defer the big money spending decision. At one time this was, in part, due to the opinion that the Suez Canal might be reopened and would therefore reduce the need for AGRY. By that time, as the fleet of VLCCs in operation exceeded 200, it no longer made any difference to AGRY if the Canal opened or not, as no VLCC could transit it. The maximum size of vessel the Canal was able to accommodate pre-closure was about 70,000 DWT. It seemed from the firm building orders of VLCC shipyards around the world that the trend would continue for tankers over 200,000 DWT for many years to come. Ship-owners and the oil industry now realized that the cheapest way to send a barrel of oil from the Arabian Gulf to Europe was in a VLCC.

On 28 July Yousuf Al-Shirawi asked me to come down to Bahrain for a general discussion. He was pleased with the progress the engineers were making, but still advocated keeping everyone keen and committed to the project, whilst cautioning me not to expect an early OAPEC decision. He doubted whether a decision would be made until a new Secretary General had been appointed.

It was interesting to find that the temperature in Bahrain at the end of July was by no means as insupportable as Jeddah. Being an island, there was a breeze, and workers in a dry dock would be in the deep canyon, with high walls on either side, in shadow except when the sun was directly overhead. Before leaving Bahrain, I had another meeting with Yousuf and he asked me to sound out Lisnave and KHI to see if

117

they would be interested in participating with OAPEC in the dry dock investment at, say, 20 per cent each. I said I would raise the matter with them, but it was doubtful either company would invest in a non-commercially viable venture, unless some other incentive could be offered to them, such as oil. He said he would think about that and discuss it when he was next in London some time during August.

On 31 July I met with Gibb/Profabril in London. They had completed the specification of AGRY and all the information contractors required to enable them to tender. Copies of these were sent to OAPEC and to Bahrain, as well as Lisnave and KHI. Things were building up to a climax of decision. However, it was impossible to force the pace of OAPEC. (Events well outside my control were formulating which would have their effect on the dry dock project.)

On 20 August I was in Lisbon to meet Mr. Perestrello. Yousuf had advised he would be in London on 23 August and asked me to invite Mr. de Mello to dine with him. In Lisbon I learned this could not be fixed as he was on a sailing holiday aboard his yacht. I was advised by Manuel Perestrello that Lisnave was not prepared to invest in AGRY, which had always been considered a national Pan-Arabic project, not structured to attract commercial investors. When Yousuf and I met in London on 23 August he was not surprised by Lisnave's reaction, but he too had become so involved with the dry dock that he could not bear to leave any stone unturned which might make it easier for OAPEC to reach the desired decision. For some time a consortium of financial institutions had been in touch with me proposing a type of lease-back financing for the OAPEC dry dock, whereby they would build it, lease it to OAPEC for 20 years, after which ownership would revert to OAPEC. The institutions were well funded and of good reputation, but the concept did not seem one which OAPEC would approve. Nevertheless, on 31 August I flew to Bahrain to discuss the matter with Yousuf. In principle, as it avoided the payment of a large sum of money at the outset, instalments being spread over 20 years, Yousuf thought it might seem a more palatable solution for OAPEC. He asked me to go to Kuwait and discuss it with the resident staff at OAPEC, which included the finance committee.

In Kuwait I had two meetings on 3 and 4 September. The additional day was needed as they wished to deliberate the proposal. On 4 September I was told that it was a possibility which gave some flexibility if members' countries were unwilling to pay up their contribution at the beginning. On 6 September I met Dr. Taher in London and discussed the financing proposal. He rejected it outright. He considered it a form of loss of OAPEC sovereignty over their own asset. They would only acquire the ownership of the dry dock after 20 years. He also considered it degrading for such wealthy states to have to resort to such means.

On 10 September Jose Manuel de Mello and Manuel Perestrello were in London and wanted to meet me to learn of any developments in AGRY from the OAPEC side. It was not possible to report anything other than a continuing keen interest. I sensed that Mr. de Mello was losing patience, but Mr. Perestrello remained positive. Mr. de Mello gave no deadline as had KHI.

I had become somewhat weary and was running out of steam, so Marcella and I left on holiday by car to the house on Elba. We spent two weeks, during which the weather was overcast and cold; we did very little swimming, a lot of walking, and returned to London feeling refreshed on 29 September.

On 5 October I made a trip to Bahrain with both John Corney and Jao Cabral, to discuss with Yousuf's Ministry the list of contractors to which it was proposed to send invitations to tender. The Ministry wanted two of the contractors' names withdrawn from the list, but otherwise 18 were acceptable. All of the tender documents were ready and the Ministry of Engineering was in a position to circulate the invitations to bid. Majid Al-Jishi, who was in charge of engineering projects in Bahrain, undertook to request permission from OAPEC to invite tenders.

Suddenly, momentous events stirred the Arab world. On 6 October Egypt and Syria attacked Israel. At first it looked as though the Arabs would win, but they were driven back largely owing, the Arabs claimed, to the sophisticated weaponry support which the US had flown out to Israel. The Arab members of OPEC succeeded in influencing the Organization to raise the price of oil to $5.12 per barrel.

On 17 October OAPEC placed an oil embargo on the United States and Holland, while implementing production cut-backs against nations considered unfriendly to the Arab cause. Meanwhile, I had returned to London on 11 October and felt that the increase in the oil price would provide OAPEC members with enlarged funds and make them more disposed to finance the dry dock. I telexed Lisnave and KHI the information about Bahrain requesting OAPEC authority to circulate invitations to tender for AGRY construction, and the fact that the oil price had increased by $2.12 per barrel. This bolstered their confidence that the project was still alive and well. It now seemed that the increase in oil prices was the stimulus which would encourage OAPEC at its next meeting to approve the dry dock project.

On Friday, 19 October, Jack Hartshorn and I met for lunch. He gave me the news that Portugal was now considered unfriendly to the Arab cause because US aircraft en route to Israel had been allowed to land at airfields in the Azores, which was a Portuguese possession. He asked whether I thought this would affect the position of Lisnave. I did not know as I had heard nothing.

After lunch I telephoned Yousuf in Bahrain. He was not very communicative on the subject, but said he was working on it and would be in

119

London on 22 October. I began to worry, because if Lisnave was no longer acceptable to OAPEC, it really meant the end of AGRY, as we could never find a suitable replacement at this point.

When I met Yousuf in London he advised me a new OAPEC Secretary General had been appointed. His name was Dr. Ali Attiga, a Libyan, who under the old regime of King Idris had been Chairman of the Libyan Insurance Company. Yousuf said he had the reputation of being very intelligent, hard working, and personable. He had completed his education in America, where he had obtained his doctorate. Yousuf then disclosed the bad news that OAPEC wanted to drop Lisnave from the project. He said they would do nothing until the next OAPEC meeting in Kuwait, which was scheduled for 5 December. By that time he hoped tempers would have cooled down, but for the present Lisnave was in a dubious position. We both agreed that Mr. Perestrello should be informed. I telephoned him and he arranged to come to London to meet with Yousuf and myself. This was probably the most difficult of all meetings relating to AGRY which had so far occurred. Yousuf explained the position by stating that the Arab world considered Portugal had acted in support of Israel by allowing US aircraft transporting arms to Israel to land in the Azores to refuel. Although no official boycott had yet been announced, if it was implemented against Portugal, Lisnave might be caught in the same net.

Manuel Perestrello, normally a calm person, was infuriated by what he considered a grossly unfair act on the part of the Arab countries, not only against Lisnave, but more particularly against Portugal. He pointed out that even had they wanted to, Portugal could not have stopped US aircraft landing in the Azores, as Portugal had leased those airfields to the Americans many years previous to the most recent Arab/Israeli war. He wanted to withdraw Lisnave from the project there and then. It became a long emotional discussion. Mr. Perestrello finally agreed that he would not withdraw Lisnave from the project, and Yousuf promised he would do all he possibly could to keep OAPEC from considering Lisnave in a political light. Lisnave had committed no unfriendly acts – no Israeli vessel had ever been docked at Lisnave. It was a very awkward moment for AGRY because, not only would a black-listing of Lisnave have been grossly unfair, we were also dealing with Portuguese pride, which in its way can be as difficult to assuage as Japanese 'loss of face'.

The respective lawyers for Lisnave, KHI and OAPEC began putting the final drafting of the Management Contract together in preparation for signing soon after the anticipated positive OAPEC decision at its December meeting. On 10 November Mr. Kawakami was in London and we met to discuss progress. It seemed that everything had been done from the side of Lisnave and KHI. The Management Contract had been agreed and was ready for signing; Gibb/Profabril had completed the engineering design; invitations to tender had now been sent out world-wide. Mr. Kawakami and I decided to have a meeting with Lisnave to discuss timing and mobilization plans. If OAPEC approved the dry dock at its December meeting, certain co-ordination with Lisnave and KHI would probably be required in appointing the contractor to build AGRY, and possibly some supervision would be needed during construction. After about 12 months, the first of the management staff would arrive to make preparations for the build-up of the eventual workforce, which should be on site in Bahrain several months before the dock became operational.

Mr. Kawakami and I met with Yousuf, who was back in London. Mr. Kawakami, mindful of the deadline of Mr. Yotsumoto, asked Yousuf if he believed that OAPEC would approve the dry dock at the December Ministerial Conference. Yousuf said he hoped so, but there were many items on the Agenda, mostly dealing with the price of oil, which kept rising. He said that in itself should give KHI confidence the dry dock would be built, as all the funds needed would now be available, even from the smallest producer in OAPEC.

Then, on Sunday, 18 November, I received a telephone call from Mr. Perestrello requesting me to come to Lisbon immediately, apologizing that he was not free to come to London because of urgent matters holding him in Lisbon. He assured me it was very important that we meet. I flew over on Sunday evening and was in his office early on Monday. He then told me about the most unbelievable blow that had yet struck AGRY. He said that a Mr. Quinas, an industrialist of considerable importance, had obtained approval from the Portuguese Government to develop land very close to Lisnave for the purpose of building a VLCC repair yard. There would be a government grant towards the construction cost, and that over the past three months Quinas had been in negotiation with KHI. The plan was that KHI would invest in the repair yard up to 40 per cent equity capital, and would manage it, using Portuguese labour. After I had recovered from the shock, I said I recalled that on my last visit to Lisbon during the week of 12 November, I had seen Mr. Hasegawa in the lobby of the Ritz, surrounded by four Portuguese business men; they shook hands and departed, and Mr. Hasegawa had walked towards the lift. I smiled and approached him, but he pretended not to see me and got into the lift. Mr. Perestrello informed me that Mr. Hasegawa had been representing KHI in the negotiations. Jose Manuel de Mello had learned of it from government sources. Mr. Perestrello said that Mr. de Mello was very upset and refused to co-operate with KHI in Bahrain and compete with them in Portugal. As far as AGRY was concerned, as Lisnave was the last one in, they would withdraw and the project could be managed by KHI.

I had been told many times that KHI would not assume an exclusive management role, and was sure this was still the case, so I asked Mr. Perestrello if Lisnave would take over the full management of the yard and perform all of the 'duties' specified in the contract. He said that if KHI withdrew, Lisnave would undertake the full management role. This really was a near catastrophe for AGRY, especially with the OAPEC meeting less than three weeks away. I told Manuel Perestrello I would try and sort it out, and would get back to him as soon as possible.

Yousuf was still in London and I saw him within an hour of my return. He was as surprised as I had been about the news, particularly as we had met with Mr. Kawakami two days previously, who had not mentioned it. He asked me if I felt Lisnave could handle the management of the dry dock alone, and I pointed out they were doing very well in Lisbon. He then asked if I had reservations about any of the duties, such as the repair of turbines or other sophisticated Japanese machinery. I felt they could handle this as they had only two Japanese engineers at Lisnave who were turbine specialists and, if necessary, Lisnave could probably acquire another two to send down to Bahrain. However, there was one area in which I saw a conflict of interest with AGRY, which was the duty of marketing the services of the yard. It would be difficult for their Marketing Division impartially to promote dockings at AGRY if Lisnave needed work. Yousuf saw this at once and said, 'Why don't you form a company to market the dry dock? You have been in since the beginning and have promoted it so far. Your company could be a partner to Lisnave, with the responsibility of all marketing "duties", such as advertising, press relations, etc.' Of course, I said I would be delighted with such a role. Yousuf then said, 'Be quick, go to see Dr. Taher and then go to Tokyo and ask KHI to either drop the Portuguese yard with Quinas, or withdraw from the OAPEC project.' Yousuf told me to fly back from Tokyo to Kuwait, to arrive there by 5 December at the latest. It was then 19 November – there should be ample time.

# 13

# NOVEMBER 1973 – JUNE 1974

Dr. Taher was able to see me in Riyadh on 24 November. He listened to a detailed disclosure of the situation. If Lisnave became the sole manager, he favoured my forming a company as party to the Management Contract which would market the repair work carried out by the dry dock. He recognized I had always been on the Arab side. He requested me to go to Tokyo to see KHI, and said he would ask OAPEC to remove the dry dock project from the Agenda of the forthcoming meeting because if there were to be changes in the management structure, it was much too late to introduce them at this stage.

On Tuesday, 27 November, Dr. Yoshida, Messrs. Hasegawa and Kawakami sat across from me at the long table. They were not flanked by any others of their team – perhaps this had no significance. I immediately introduced the subject by saying that Mr. de Mello and Mr. Perestrello were very upset when they learned from the government of KHI's plans to build a ship-repair yard near Lisnave in conjunction with Quinas interests. Mr. de Mello felt KHI should have disclosed this information to him, and he was not now prepared to co-operate with KHI in Bahrain and compete in Portugal. I said that Mr. de Mello had offered to withdraw Lisnave from the AGRY project as KHI had been identified with it for a longer time. I then said that OAPEC wished to know if KHI would undertake the full dry dock management role. Dr. Yoshida replied that KHI had said many times this would not be possible. I then asked if they would drop the Quinas venture so that they could continue to share the management role with Lisnave. Mr. Hasegawa said KHI could not do this, and went on to say he could not understand Mr. de Mello's attitude. This provoked me to ask how KHI would feel if Lisnave were to find Japanese partners and cause a new building yard to be created next to Sakaide. Mr. Hasegawa replied, 'Ah, we would help them.' Dr. Yoshida then said it would be correct for KHI to withdraw from the OAPEC project.

They provided a car to drive me back to the hotel; I packed, caught the JAL flight back to London and arrived on 29 November. I wrote to KHI saying that with regret I would inform OAPEC of their withdrawal.

I also communicated with Dr. Taher, Yousuf and Mr. Perestrello. I did not wish to make a further trip to Lisbon as there was nothing I could say until the matter had been discussed with Dr. Taher and Yousuf, whom I would meet in Kuwait.

On 4 December I flew to Kuwait and on 5 December met Dr. Ali Attiga for the first time. He was very likeable, with a vital personality. His initial question was to ask why Dr. Taher had requested that the dry dock project be removed from the Agenda of Saturday's meeting. I did not know how much had been said about Lisnave/KHI, so I replied that it had been considered more useful to have all the bids in from the contractors so that OAPEC would receive a more accurate picture of the building cost and we would not have to come back a second time for its approval. Dr. Attiga welcomed the delay because the price of oil would occupy most of the OAPEC meeting time. He said the Shah of Iran was demanding $20 a barrel for oil, and that Sheikh Yamani was opposed to such a price increase from its October OPEC $5.12 level. Dr. Attiga said he anticipated Sheikh Yamani would try and convince his OAPEC colleagues to agree on a more moderate increase to, perhaps, $10 per barrel. Dr. Attiga differed from his predecessor, in that he was extremely well informed about the dry dock, even to the names of individuals involved.

The next two days were very busy ones for the OAPEC delegates, with a great deal of private meetings and a flow of traffic in and out of Sheikh Yamani's suite. Jack Hartshorn was in Kuwait covering the meeting for his oil consultancy firm. The meeting agreed on a united stand of $10 per barrel to present to the next OPEC meeting to be held in a few days. $10 per barrel produced more than three times the income of the OAPEC states when they had started to consider AGRY and this should make financing the dry dock easier for them.

In spite of the busy time, I was able to have a word with Sheikh Yamani, who knew of the dry dock developments and confirmed his continued support. I had longer talks with Dr. Taher and Yousuf, who were quite pleased with developments, which left only Lisnave, and both wished me luck in my talks with Mr. de Mello about assigning the marketing duties to a company I would form.

Jack Hartshorn and I left Kuwait on 9 December for Beirut and the Hotel St. George. The next day we went over to the offices of the Middle East Economic Survey and met the Editors, Fuad Itayim and Ian Seymour. It was very interesting listening to those expert petroleum economists trying to predict the outcome of the next OPEC pricing battle between the two most influential OPEC Ministers, the charismatic Sheikh Yamani, and the cold pragmatic Minister of the Shah, Yamshid Amouzegar.

On Friday, 14 December, Mr. de Mello and Mr. Perestrello met me in Lisbon. Mr. de Mello asked if Lisnave was boycotted, and I was pleased to tell him that OAPEC had taken no such action. I said that Dr. Taher and Yousuf Al-Shirawi were prepared to propose Lisnave management of the dry dock with the exclusion of those duties in respect to marketing, advertising, and all promotional duties specified in the contract, which would be carried out by a company to be formed and managed by me. I was able to return to London the same day by the evening flight. Not much could be done until I heard from Jose Manuel de Mello, and in any case the year had progressed to the Christmas season.

I heard from Yousuf that he had received an official letter of withdrawal from KHI. Sheikh Yamani had won a victory for the moderates in OPEC by patiently opposing the Shah's call for an oil price rise to $20 per barrel. The price was eventually settled at $11.65 per barrel, much nearer to Sheikh Yamani's $10 proposal.

On Boxing Day the telephone rang. It was Jose Manuel de Mello to say that as both Lisnave and the marketing company would be associated in the management role, we should push things along a bit faster. Lisnave had been working so far on AGRY for 18 months. How much longer before we could expect OAPEC's decision? I said that it was my guess OAPEC would decide to proceed with AGRY during a meeting in 1974. A year's delay had been mainly due on OAPEC's side to the large amount of money each member would have to contribute as a grant to the project to cover its construction cost. During the past year the price of oil had almost quadrupled, which must make OAPEC states less reluctant to invest capital in the dry rock. Mr. de Mello said, 'Let's hope so.'

On 28 December I airfreighted a report to Dr. Taher in the Kingdom and one to Yousuf in Bahrain. I also met with my solicitors, Freshfields, to request them to amend the Management Contract to incorporate a company to be formed by me, to assume all of the related marketing 'duties'.

In years to come, when looking back on what must appear as the twentieth-century Arab renaissance, what will be remembered from that period of uncontrolled growth? It will not be considered as significant as that seventh-century Arab expansion, which occurred within 100 years of the life of Mohammed. On that occasion the Arab world stretched from Tours in France, to Canton in China, and an Arab merchant could cash his cheque, drawn on a bank in Damascus, anywhere in the Arab area of influence, whilst contemporary European monarchs kept their money under the bed and wondered at these Islamic people who discovered the zero in mathematics, algebra and logarithms, and yet mostly ignored the visual arts. What were the achievements in this century? A benign king remarked in 1973 that the oil wealth would be sufficient to feed the Muslim populations throughout the world, only to be inhibited by his religious advisers, who first asked him if he wanted to be God, which he denied. They then told him to stop acting like God, because if it was God's wish that other Muslims should eat, he would feed them. So instead of fighting hunger, they decided to industrialize in an attempt to divert from a one-resource economy. In the late 1970s monuments began to appear in the desert (albeit less durable than the pyramids), as various industrial plants competed for sites with ultra-modern hospitals, technical universities, airports and hotels. Whole new towns were built, providing housing for 50,000 with infrastructure of schools, hospitals, etc. A town was created in the desert, giving the feeling of a Nomadic Bedouin settlement, which would fold tents and depart, leaving no mark as the desert reclaimed man's construction. A few of the structures of industrialization gave good service, such as refineries, petrochemical installations, and desalination plants. It is remarkable that such new-found wealth did not more adversely affect the young educated, Saudis, Kuwaitis and others, amongst the large petroleum producers. Of course, men like Sheikh Yamani and Dr. Taher were so evolved that to them it only appeared as the vehicle on which Saudi Arabia could emerge from its desert Kingdom status. The Arab Semitic mind is a very flexible instrument. Most of the young meritocrats whom I met seemed more intelligent and wiser than their western counterparts. To start with, when they spoke English, it was with a greater fluency and less accent than most Germans, French or Italians, and, of course, it was much more of an achievement with a different alphabet and even a different way of reading, which was from right to left across the page. They grasped new ideas with alacrity, although some concepts eluded them entirely.

Marcella and I celebrated New Year's Eve at Annabel's, and hoped that 1974 would see AGRY approval without any more upheavals.

On Friday, 4 January 1974, in answer to a request from Yousuf, I flew down to Bahrain. My frequent referral to the Minister of Development, Yousuf Al-Shirawi, as 'Yousuf' might need explaining. Unless on official occasions, where representing the Ruler of Bahrain, it was his request to all persons having business dealings with him to address him as 'Yousuf' rather than the formal 'Your Excellency'. The reason was never made clear, but probably had its roots in the Bedouin informality of the desert where everyone is known by his first name – the second name merely denoting the tribe to which he belonged. It was still true that a Bedouin from the Saudi desert would address King Faisal at his Majlis merely as 'Faisal' when making his needs known, such as, another female camel for his herd, etc.

Yousuf wanted to discuss the Management Contract, and how we intended to incorporate the assignment of the marketing duties. He also expressed the view that, although KHI had contributed a great deal towards the evolution of the dry dock, it would be easier with the management being handled only by Lisnave, than the mixed team with its language barriers. He told me to tell Lisnave he was optimistic about OAPEC approving the scheme during 1974.

I arrived back in London on Sunday, 6 January. The next day I flew to Geneva, where Sheikh Yamani was involved in an OPEC meeting. More meetings were now being held in the Intercontinental Hotel in Geneva, rather than at OPEC headquarters in Vienna. Communications between Switzerland and the Kingdom were better than from Austria.

On 8 January I was able to have a short meeting with Sheikh Yamani. He had been brought completely up-to-date with developments, and his support continued. On behalf of Mr. de Mello, I asked when he thought OAPEC would approve the dry dock project. He replied, 'At the next full Ministerial Conference, to take place in 1974.' I flew to Lisbon to tell Mr. de Mello this news in person.

After my return to London, Yousuf telephoned to say he was arriving the following day, and invited me to attend an interesting test which John Corney was carrying out at the Wimpey Laboratory. A large model of the reclaimed dry dock site was reproduced in the Wimpey test tank, where simulated waves and tidal action could be observed and their effect on the dry dock island/causeway could be calculated. This was the first time any of us got a clear impression of how the dry dock site would look, and the length of the causeway to Al Hidd. The test was positive, even to determining the amount of silting. An excellent photograph was taken of Yousuf, John Corney and all of us, staring over the expanse of water in the tank to the man-made island, where the dry dock would be situated, as though waiting for a VLCC to come over the horizon. We had a celebratory lunch and Yousuf voiced the opinion that the worst was over. I intoned the Arab phrase, 'Im sh Allah', which is frequently used and means 'if God wills it'.

Lisnave wanted to make new calculations and cash flows, because the picture had altered as KHI would not be providing the turbine technicians and other machinery experts. These would now come from Lisbon, and instead of being on a 3–6 month rota, would be on a permanent basis, with home leave after two years. This required slight adjustments to the operating costs, happily for the better. I agreed to come over to Lisbon and help Lisnave, if not with the technical details, then with the presentation of what was to become yet another feasibility study for OAPEC.

Mr. de Mello owned a large hotel in the Algarve on Portugal's southern coast, by the name of the Alvor. In February the hotel was open, but had very few guests. He invited Marcella and me to spend a week there, and Lisnave would send Mr. Carreira down from time to time when my help was needed on the study. Because of the action of the Gulf Stream, the Algarve has full spring in February, with mimosa, almond blossoms and wild flowers in bloom. We drove down to the hotel on Saturday, 2 February. The Alvor was less than five years old, quite large, situated on the edge of a cliff, with a very long beach below. It was pleasant to be amongst only five guests off season (which is the best time in a well run and extremely comfortable hotel).

In February the Algarve weather passes rapidly from warm sun to strong wind, showers, and back to sun. We were on the Atlantic coast and there was no mistaking the smell of iodine or the strength of the breakers, so different from the adjacent Mediterranean around the point. Every other afternoon, Mr. Carreira, with one or two of his team, would fly down to the nearby private landing strip in an aircraft of the de Mello Group. We would then go into one of the empty reception rooms and work on the feasibility study. As previously mentioned, my work mostly related to presentation and semantics. It was, I believe, the most congenial ambiance in which I ever engaged in serious work. Lisnave were very conscientious and it is probable that OAPEC never received a more polished or fine-honed study, down to the cover which portrayed an early Portuguese map used by one of its fifteenth-century navigators who had established a fort on Bahrain. The fort is still standing, and is known in both English and Arabic as the Portuguese fort. It is one of the tourist attractions of Bahrain, where one can still pick up shards of blue and white pottery that Portuguese ships had brought from China.

As there were no lights on the landing strip, just before dark the Lisnave explorers would take off for Lisbon. This occurred three times during the week we were at the Alvor. We only had breakfast in the hotel, and would investigate the fish restaurants in the nearby villages. Each time we left the hotel, we were surprised to find the many flowers and blossoms which even the South of France could not offer in February. On Monday, 11 February, we returned to Lisbon where I spent Tuesday and Wednesday at Lisnave. We left on Thursday morning with 25 copies of the feasibility study stacked in the back of the car.

In London I had the pleasure of seeing Peter Nash again. He had become a partner in A. & P. Appledore, and had designed the huge Korean VLCC new building shipyard at Ulsan. The occasion was a large luncheon at the Savoy, given by the Chairman of Hyundai, the owners of the shipyard. Peter Nash still remembered arriving at Jeddah during the Hajj.

Dr. Serra Lopes came over to London to meet with John Kennedy, who was acting for OAPEC on the Management Contract in its revised form. At the beginning of March, Yousuf came to London for a meeting with John Corney to try and hurry up some of the contractors, whose bids had not yet been received in Bahrain. The bids were kept sealed in a government safe and would all be opened on the same day.

On 7 April I flew to Bahrain to attend the bid-opening ceremony. Representatives of Sir Alexander Gibb, Profabril and Lisnave were all present. Nine companies had tendered. What would then follow was the long process of bid evaluation, comparing time and cost for the various sections of the tender. This could take a couple of weeks. I returned to London the next day.

There was a series of meetings with Mr. Perestrello, the lawyers about the Management Contract, the engineers about the tender evaluation, all of which were really perfunctory – everyone was waiting for OAPEC – all of the work had been done as far as presenting a package on which OAPEC could make its decision. Yousuf had to be in Zurich on 25 April and he wanted a word with Manuel Perestrello, so it was arranged that we would all meet at the Hotel Dolder for dinner. However, Manuel Perestrello did not turn up because he had been tied up and locked in his office by the Lisnave workers on the morning of 25 April, when the Portuguese Revolution took place and the Dictator Caetano was overthrown. He could not telephone to let us know. Yousuf and I had dinner alone, having received no word from Mr. Perestrello, but having learned of the Revolution. At that time we did not know it had been bloodless, but we heard it was communist inspired. We sat glumly over dinner, wondering whether the death blow had been struck to the OAPEC dry dock venture. Certainly, OAPEC would not accept that a communist country would operate its dry dock. Yousuf and I flew back to London, where he transferred to a flight to Bahrain. I promised to go to Lisbon as soon as I could and to telephone him the latest news.

On Tuesday, 30 April, Mr. Perestrello telephoned me. The situation was not normal, but not nearly as bad as the press had indicated. There were still some strikes, but the one at Lisnave in which he had been locked up was over, and they had just docked another VLCC that morning. The country had changed from a dictatorship to a republic with a socialist president. The government had plans to nationalize a number of banks and insurance companies, but not Lisnave because of its 40% Dutch and Swedish shareholding. I invited Mr. Perestrello to a meeting of the Middle East Association which would be held at the Guildhall on 8 May. Both Sheikh Yamani and Yousuf were to be speakers. He accepted with pleasure and I was delighted to be able to exhibit him, alive and well, after the Revolution. It would reassure Sheikh Yamani and Yousuf.

Yousuf flew over on 7 May. I met him at the airport and was happy to tell him that nothing had happened in Portugal which would mitigate against Lisnave managing the OAPEC dry dock. He was pleased that Mr. Perestrello was to attend the meeting the following day.

Mr. Perestrello and I got to the Guildhall early and were lucky to find seats in the front row of the conference hall. There were four speakers before the coffee break. The last one was Yousuf, who spoke about the dry dock and introduced Sheikh Yamani, who would be the first speaker when the meeting resumed. We were seated when Sheikh Yamani took his position at the speakers' desk. He smiled in his charismatic way and had the whole room with him. At the buffet lunch, I introduced Manuel

Perestrello to him and they exchanged a few words. In my opinion, the dry dock became alive for Manuel Perestrello after that meeting. In the afternoon there was a reception at the Hyde Park Hotel, Mr. Perestrello met Dr. Ali Attiga and had a chance for a longer talk with Sheikh Yamani, during which they discussed the dry dock. Sheikh Yamani said he welcomed the project as a step towards industrialization in the Arabian Peninsular.

The following day Yousuf, Mr. Perestrello and I flew to Lisbon. Yousuf wanted to see the situation for himself. We dined with Mr. Perestrello, together with John Corney, Jao Cabral and Mr. Carreira. Apart from graffiti and posters, Portugal's Flower Revolution seemed to have altered the surface of Lisbon very little. (It was called the Flower Revolution because the military, which had been called out, had stuck red carnations in the muzzles of their guns, which they had not been required to fire.) Yousuf returned to Bahrain via London, and I stayed on for another day to visit Lisnave and observe if any apparent change in the workers' attitude had occurred. There was none I could see, but it must surely have existed, as the animosity directed towards Mr. Perestrello and the ensuing strike could not be forgotten from one day to the next. However, the managers of the yard said that work had not slowed down, and the same efficiency which had existed pre-revolution prevailed.

We returned to waiting for an OAPEC meeting so that a decision could be taken. My lawyer had meetings with the Lisnave lawyer on the Management Contract, but all forward motion had stopped, as nothing more could be done until OAPEC made its decision. The evaluation of the tender documents had been completed. The Korean firm of Hyundai had been the most competitive, both in price and time. On 14 June I flew down to Bahrain at Yousuf's request. He told me that the OAPEC Ministerial Conference would take place in Cairo on 10 July and asked me to bring 25 copies of the Management Contract. This news was passed on to Lisnave and Gibb/Profabril. One effect of the Portuguese Revolution was that Quinas decided not to build the shiprepair yard in Lisbon – I learned this from Mr. Kawakami, who very much regretted that it was now too late to join in again with AGRY.

# 14

# JUNE 1974 – DECEMBER 1976

Sheikh Yamani was in London for discussions with the British Minister of Energy and on 22 June had tea with us at home. He remarked to Marcella that he always drank very weak tea or coffee for stomach reasons. She said she did too. Sheikh Yamani observed that he believed in natural remedies, rather than prescribed drugs, and recommended papaya pills.

At last the day for departure to Cairo arrived on 8 July. Yousuf and his lawyer, Donald Jones, the Petromin lawyer, John Kennedy, and I had dinner that evening at the Nile Hilton, where the OAPEC meeting would be held on 10 July. The Hilton was fully booked by delegates and their staff. Rooms had been reserved for the fringe players across the Nile at the Sheraton. Accommodation had been obtained there at the last moment for Manuel Perestrello and Dr. Serra Lopes, who had advised on 7 July that they would be attending. Only my lawyer from Freshfields was absent, and I hoped legal advice would not be required. At about midnight, John Kennedy, Donald Jones and I walked across the bridge to the Sheraton. It was a very hot night and it would have been pleasant to use the outdoor swimming pool, but it was closed.

The next day, for diversion from the anxious hours of waiting, Yousuf suggested a visit to the pyramids. Yousuf has long been interested in archaeology and had made a study of the third millenium BC, during which the Dilman civilization flourished – the first inhabitants of Bahrain. We had all seen the pyramids before, but Yousuf made this visit more interesting because of his knowledge. That night we had a sort of working buffet dinner in Yousuf's suite and were joined by Sheikh Khalifa. Yousuf questioned John Kennedy and Donald Jones on the Management Contract, and me on the market potential for the dry dock – how many ships we expected to repair per year, types of repair, cost of simple maintenance docking to improve the VLCC speed and performance, etc. We argued about every question Yousuf might be asked the next day.

This time it was 2:30 when John Kennedy, Donald James and I crossed the bridge to the Sheraton. In the lobby there was a familiar shape trying to get comfortable on a sofa. It was Manuel Perestrello, and on another

131

sofa I spotted Dr. Serra Lopes. They had arrived and were told 'there was no room at the inn'. After some discussion and persuasion, two rooms were found for them. They were pretty travel worn as their flight had been cancelled, which meant proceeding slowly, changing aircraft at almost each stop – Paris, Madrid, Rome and Athens – with a resultant loss of luggage somewhere *en route*.

On the morning of 10 July we were part of the crowd of press and others who watched the OAPEC Ministers enter the conference room. Sheikh Yamani spotted me, walked over, reached into his pocket and pulled out two bottles of papaya pills. He said, 'Tell your wife to take two each day, they are natural enzymes.' What an extraordinarily thoughtful gesture from such a busy world figure!

The meeting finished by lunch time. All those awaiting the outcome of the meeting were sitting on sofas ranged around the ante-room. The doors opened and Sheikh Yamani emerged, accompanied by Dr. Ali Attiga. They were immediately surrounded by press. I caught the eye of Sheikh Yamani and he nodded in the affirmative. The dry dock had been approved! My first reaction was that now the marketing work would begin and we had to start courting that first ship. Later, we heard the details from Yousuf. OAPEC had approved awarding the construction contract to Hyundai and had authorized the signing of the Management Contract.

The following day, 11 July, the Contract was signed by Dr. Taher, Yousuf Al-Shirawi, Manuel Perestrello and myself. Everyone, except Donald Jones and me, left Cairo. That night Donald and I had a quiet meal in the coffee shop of the Sheraton. The next morning I flew Swissair to Zurich, where Marcella met me at the Hotel Dolder. We were in Zurich to celebrate my uncle's 85th birthday.

On 17 July I asked Mike Ratcliffe to lunch and offered him the job as Managing Director of the London based company to be formed to market the services of the dry dock, of which I would be Chairman. We agreed terms at which he was prepared to give up his job and directorship with H. P. Drewry. He would give three months' notice and be able to join me on Monday, 18 October. Both Mike and I remained friends with the H. P. Drewry organization, subscribing to their publication and using their services on special economic studies.

It was now clear an office had to be found, a company formed, a secretary employed for Mike, as well as arranging for telex and telephones, stationery and other necessary equipment, which seemed rather a lot of pieces to put together by 18 October.

On 18 July I met with Freshfields and caused the company to be formed, but was unable to decide on a name, which I asked to be delayed for a couple of weeks. I flew to Lisbon on Sunday for a meeting with Lisnave in order to arrive at a clear understanding of our respective duties under the Management Contract. It was agreed that the company would promote the services of the yard, working through a world-wide agency network, with agents located in each shipping centre. It would, through its agents, sell a docking, but Lisnave on behalf of AGRY would establish the price and sign the repair contract. I returned to London on Tuesday, 23 July, happy that there was no disagreement with Lisnave on the question of duties. An office was found on Pall Mall in a good building.

On 1 August I flew down to Bahrain to discuss the name of the marketing company with Yousuf, and, more importantly, the name of the dry dock. Yousuf said that because Iran was a member of OPEC, and the body of water separating it from the Arabian Peninsular had for years been called the Persian Gulf, and was so referred to in all the marine atlases and Admiralty charts, Sheikh Yamani felt it would be offensive to Iran to call the dry dock Arabian Gulf Repair Yard, suggesting that the Arabs had taken over that body of water. We discussed possible names for a short while and Yousuf put forward the name Arab Shipbuilding and Repair Yard, with the initials spelling ASRY, and this was the name by which the dry dock became known world-wide. Of course, it was obvious that the London-based company should be named 'Arab Shipbuilding and Repair Yard Marketing Services Limited', or ASRYMAR. It was a good name, as ASRYMAR combined both marketing and marine connotations.

The small details of establishing an office, such as having stationery printed, visiting cards for Mike and myself, occupied the next two weeks. Dredging work had started in Bahrain and under Hyundai things were progressing fast. In October Mike joined ASRYMAR and from the beginning he made a significant contribution. His background as an economist, and his familiarity with statistical work, soon had him sorting out by owner, building date, last docking date, office from which the ship was operated, every VLCC afloat, as well as other files on all VLCC's on order. The yard would become operational by December 1977, and from a world fleet of over 500 VLCCs and ULCCs in service by that date, he had narrowed down to 50 ships from which the inaugural vessel for docking would come. He plotted statistics on a 12, 18 and 24 month docking cycle. Perhaps readers will find this boring, so suffice it to say he brought modern technology to ship-repair yard marketing.

Yousuf had advised that the cornerstone-laying ceremony would take place on 30 November, and asked for a small list of guests whom he should invite from the shipping and press world. It was planned that the Ruler would lay the cornerstone. Speeches would be made by the Prime Minister, Sheikh Yamani and Yousuf. Lisnave had arranged to make a large model of ASRY which would be enclosed by a glass showcase. It was a very realistic model, with water in the dock and a VLCC moored at the bow. Yousuf asked ASRYMAR to order 50 silver cigarette boxes with the yard in relief on the lid as gifts to selected guests. There were also gifts for the press and for all who attended the ceremony. This caused some toing and froing between Lisnave and ASRYMAR and Bahrain, but everyone was enthusiastic, co-operative, and determined to make ASRY and all its functions a success.

On 23 November Marcella and I flew to Bahrain. The sun shone after rainy London and the temperature was a pleasant 18°C. Lisnave, Gibb/Profabril, Hyundai's people and I were quite busy with different tasks for the next week. Yousuf gave a large dinner party on the 25th and other evenings were spent with various acquaintances we had in Bahrain, such as Ahmed Kanoo, and James Belgrave, who published the English language newspaper – the *Gulf Mirror*. He was the son of the late Sir Charles Belgrave, who had become the most important British resident in Bahrain. He had been the link with the West on all matters to the present Ruler's father. Charles Belgrave was an officer in the Brigade of Guards when, immediately after the First World War, he saw an advertisement in *The Times* for an 'experienced English gentleman to act as advisor to the Ruler of an Arabian Sheikdom'. He came and stayed for more than 30 years until his death. James still lived in the same colonial-style house, built to his father's design. Having been a British protectorate, a number of strange and colourful expatriates have been attracted to the island, such as the monolithic Ralph Izzard, the last man out of the *The Times* Berlin office when the Second World War broke out. He was a great friend of Kim Philby and saw him often when Philby worked for the *Observer* in Beirut. Philby's son comes down to Bahrain to stay with him. In spite of his height, he was a noted mountaineer and climbed in the Himalayas. In 1974 he worked as a cameraman for Viznews in Bahrain, and it was an awesome sight to see him lean far out of the door of a helicopter in order to get a better shot of ASRY.

On the afternoon of 30 November we all went over to the site of the new causeway through which the ASRY island would be linked. All the Ministerial members of OAPEC, its Secretary General, Dr. Ali Attiga, members of the ruling family, Messrs. de Mello and Perestrello from Lisnave, a few oil company representatives and a dozen or so of the Middle East reporters of the more important shipping and financial journals were present. All were gathered under a multi-coloured canopy. The cornerstone was cemented into place by His Highness Sheikh Isa. It was very close to the large model of the shipyard in its glass case. After the Prime Minister, Sheikh Yamani made a speech. He cut a romantic figure with his Arab headdress and robes blowing in the wind. After the ceremony we all returned to the guest palace, where the Ruler provided a banquet for all of the male guests. The women had their own dinner party, given by Mai Shirawi, Yousuf's wife. After so many years it was hard to believe that ASRY was being built and due to be completed less than three years hence.

On Sunday, 1 December, I was asked to address a rotary meeting being held in Bahrain, and give a history of ASRY to date. The problem was to keep it short!

John Corney and his wife, Joan, Marcella and I, flew to Beirut to spend a pleasant night at the St. George, and left the next morning for Cairo. Marcella had never been to Cairo. We spent two nights at the Sheraton, visited the 'son et lumière' in the presence of the sphinx and the large pyramid of Cheops, a very moving display, the text being spoken by Jean Louis Barrault. Three languages were broadcast on successive nights – French, English and Arabic. On Wednesday morning we found a very erudite guide who was fluent in English and visited the area of the pyramids, entered some tomb chambers and were well taught by this informed guide, who we asked to remain with us for the rest of the day while we visited the Mohammed Ali Mosque, and the museum of Egyptology. This last was the most casually kept treasure one had ever seen. A few years previously it was possible to acquire important Pharaonic relics by haggling with the guards. This had changed by the time we got there, although it still remained badly lighted and poorly laid out.

On 5 December we were back in London. ASRY had been launched and we had three years in which to convince discriminating shipowners of its capabilities, and to instil enough confidence in them to put their ships in an untried dock in a part of the world removed from engineering back-up help if anything went wrong. This would prove less difficult to achieve than the ups and downs which led to the OAPEC decision to build ASRY. ASRY could never have been achieved without the steadfast support of Sheikh Yamani. As prospective managers withdrew, or were dismissed, there arose seven distinct occasions when the majority of OAPEC members were in favour of abandoning what they considered a crazy project, an investment on which they would never recover their money. It was Sheikh Yamani's patient belief in the project as the first Pan-Arabic industrial venture, with its technological transfer and overall educational contribution that each time convinced OAPEC to stay a little longer. Finally, through his oil diplomacy, Sheikh Yamani provided OAPEC revenues beyond the oil producers' wildest dreams, and made their investment in ASRY painless.

On Sunday, 8 December, I met Sheikh Yamani and Dr. Taher at the Carlton Tower Hotel in London. They were no longer involved in ASRY, beyond their continuing wish to see it succeed. ASRY, as a company, was being formed with Saudi Arabia, Kuwait, Bahrain, Qatar and United Arab Emirates investors. Libya and Iraq had applied to join OAPEC, as both countries qualified as oil was their principal source of revenue. Each made a small investment in ASRY, but not equal to that of the original five founder members.

Marcella and I celebrated the close of 1974 at a friend's house.

On 4 January 1975 I flew to Bahrain – the team of Lisnave and ASRYMAR had been invited to attend ASRY's first Board Meeting. We all stayed at the Gulf Hotel. There was a tremendous air of excitement and resolve towards the brand new ASRY. The Board Meeting was not scheduled until the 7th, when ASRY's first Chairman would be appointed. However, there were several matters we wanted to sort out before the meeting. ASRY needed an office until its own administration building was erected on site. It had to be fairly large, as about 40 staff would be at work dealing with procurement, engineering, recruitment and financial services. Until the Board met, no signatories had been nominated, and the lease for the office could not be signed. We had found three suitable office locations of similar size, but at differing priced rentals. The selection would be one of the Board's first tasks.

We had a meeting with Yousuf, who was pleased to see the commencement of activity on behalf of ASRY. We went by boat to the site, where Hyundai were busily forming the ASRY island from reclaimed land which two large dredgers were sucking up from the sea floor.

On Tuesday morning, 7 January, Mr. Carreira and I arrived at Government House, where the Board Meeting was to be held (in the cabinet room loaned for the purpose). As the members came in we were introduced to them. Each of the investing OAPEC countries had sent a member and an alternate. Very young men from Saudi Arabia, Kuwait, Bahrain, Qatar, United Arab Emirates, Iraq and Libya entered the room, not quite knowing what to expect. Only three of them had previously visited Bahrain. However, all of them spoke reasonably fluent English. They had been recruited from the petroleum ministries of their respective countries. They were all intelligent, but Mr. Carreira and I had the impression that none of them knew what a dry dock was supposed to do, or why it should be doing it. On the other hand, they could certainly teach us a lot of things about oil production. They soon grasped that the two were related. The seven representatives of the investing Arab States commenced their Board Meeting. We waited in an ante-room to be summoned. The Board Meeting was, of course, conducted in Arabic except when the management team was called in to provide the Board with information which was given in English. The Board members came out after about an hour for a refreshment break. They had appointed Majid Al-Jishi (Yousuf's Deputy) as Chairman. There were two reasons for this – the next two years would contain a number of engineering decisions, and Majid was the only engineer amongst them. The other reason was that he was a Bahraini and therefore available in Bahrain when matters affecting ASRY had to be dealt with on a day-to-day basis, especially those requiring approval of various government departments, such as Customs, Port Authority, electricity and other services.

After the break, the Board called in Mr. Carreira and myself. The Chairman asked Mr. Carreira to explain Lisnave's role to the Board. He did this in a comprehensive way, describing the initial supervisory work during construction and the subsequent duties when the yard became operational. The Board asked Mr. Carreira to prepare a budget of costs for duties carried out during 1975. I was asked to explain the marketing duties of ASRYMAR. These were more difficult for them to understand, as no marketing function was associated with their sales of oil, which in the case of most states, only had one customer. It seemed that they had come to believe ASRY would be so necessary to shipowners coming to the Gulf, that no selling effort would be required. A long discussion ensued, which drew the differences between marketing and selling. The work that was essential to introduce a new shiprepair yard and to instil shipowner confidence in a completely untried facility, in a part of the world not identified with ship-repairing, was explained. As they were intelligent, they were able to comprehend a concept that was new to them and asked if I believed it would be possible to find a ship-owner to be the first to put his ship into ASRY's dry dock. I tried to assure them that we would. I was also asked to submit a budget of ASRYMAR's operating costs for the current year. I showed them a logo symbol for ASRY which Mike Ratcliffe had designed. It was a circle, representing the globe, which had at its centre and across the diameter the profile of a dry dock. The bottom half was in the colour of the red lead antifouling paint used on ships below the waterline, the top half of the circle being coloured black, which was the colour most ships were painted above the waterline. The Board liked it, and in due course ASRY's log became well known amongst ship-owners.

The Board approved the leasing of the most expensive of the three office proposals, and said it would hold its next meeting in the new premises on 3 February, after which we all had lunch together. It was about three in the afternoon, and as all the business of the meeting had not been completed, it was agreed to continue the following day. Mr Carreira suggested the Board might wish to visit the site following the next day's meeting. All members were keen to do this. The next day we all went out to the ASRY site, about a half hour boat ride from Bahrain's commercial port as the causeway had not yet been built. All that was visible was the small round island, except for the huge pipes pouring out wet material from the sea bed on to the island. Dutch dredgers worked continuously, with accommodation for their crews on board.

One had the impression that all of this was a new and interesting experience for the young Board members, most of whom were in their early twenties. Of course, this did not apply to Majid Al-Jishi, a very experienced civil engineer, who had been involved in much of the development work in Bahrain sparked off by Yousuf, such as roads, electricity generating stations, and the airport extension. After returning to the mainland, we said goodbye to the Board members. Mr. Carreira stayed in Bahrain to get the office lease signed by the Chairman, and to go about finding furniture, office equipment, telex and telephones, etc., and I returned to London.

Mike Ratcliffe and I started to prepare our 1975 budget, based on an advertising campaign and other PR material, such as gifts bearing the ASRY logo, which ASRY agents would distribute to marine superintendents in shipowners' offices. Those items were not costly, but chosen with care so as to be useful reminders of ASRY – pens, diaries, lighters, a silk tie woven with the ASRY logo, etc. Two large receptions per year were planned in major shipowning areas – in 1975 these were held in Oslo and London.

We started a monthly magazine known as ASRYNEWS. The front page was prepared for us by a professional journalist who had a background with the *Financial Times*. It dealt with news of economic and business interests in the Arabian Gulf. The centre pages dealt with ship-repair news around the world, and on the back page were quite comprehensive shipping statistics of interest to tanker and dry cargo trades.

There is nothing exciting, or even unique, in any of the many devices ASRYMAR employed to make ASRY well known more than two years before it could repair its first ship. What was unusual was that such an old, unlively industry as ship-repairing should have at its disposal a vast budget to spend world-wide to make its existence known. The results certainly proved the importance of marketing.

One of the things ASRYMAR did invent, and which was adopted by other shipyards, was the 'economic' docking. This consisted of a short three-day docking, during which the hull and vessel bottom were cleaned and painted, tail shaft and sea valves examined and propeller inspected. It was called 'economic' because it provided a financial benefit to the ship-owner. It was estimated that from 1 to 2 knots service speed were lost through friction drag caused by a dirty hull fouled by marine growth. At various tanker rates (world scale), 1 knot service speed lost meant a financial loss over a year which could be as high as $900,000 worth of carrying capacity to a VLCC shipowner. Clearly, the slower the ship, the fewer loaded pay knots a VLCC could voyage per year. From its first year ASRYNEWS carried graphs showing the financial loss at current charter rates of lost speed calibrated in 0.10 knots up to 2 full knots. The cleaned hull results showed savings two to three times greater than the cost of the 'economic' docking.

The 'economic' docking had another advantage for ASRY as it was the easiest and quickest kind of repair docking a new shipyard could perform, requiring far less accumulated skills than the full-fledged docking ASRY was later able to carry out. ASRY's location was also ideal, because when it became operational there were always about 25–30 VLCCs a few miles distant in the queue waiting to load at Ras Tanura, the Aramco oil terminal in Saudi Arabia. In the first two or three years after ASRY became operational, other VLCC yards were not keen to take on economic dockings, preferring large survey repairs which would employ their skilled workforce and produce a much higher invoice – up to ten times the price of an economic docking.

ASRYMAR arranged for a colour film to be produced by Viznews which showed ASRY being built, glimpses of the Arab world, introductions to key managers and repair divisional heads, as well as other audovisual material of interest which had been compressed into a 15–minute presentation which was updated every three months. This ensured that ASRY agents were almost never turned away when they appeared at a shipowner's office with their portable machine to show the ASRY film, which became a serial in quarterly instalments up to ASRY's inauguration. By then it had been shown in the office of every VLCC owning company in the world. Viznews did a good job of producing this documentary. David Brower, who was in charge of production, made many trips to Bahrain, together with his camera team. As I write of this period some thirteen and a half years ago, I recall all the enthusiasm and energy which Lisnave and ASRYMAR expended to make ASRY a credit to its investors.

When I returned to Bahrain at the end of January for the February Board Meeting, I was in admiration of the speedy equipping of the ASRY office. In three weeks, each of the 20 rooms, and a large Boardroom, had been furnished, carpeted, with telephones, telexes and Xeroxes, installed. There was also a large machine for reproducing plans and engineering drawings. It would have been difficult to assemble that in Europe within the same time-scale.

Lisnave had appointed a British financial manager, an Arab personnel manager, a British production manager and a Portuguese general manager who was ex-Lisnave, all reporting to Mr. Carreira.

On 2 February ASRY had its Annual General Meeting preceding the Board Meeting. Lisnave and ASRYMAR budgets were approved and the Board complimented Lisnave on the ASRY office arrangements. The Board table could seat 20. Mr. Carreira said he had been amazed at the facilities Bahrain offered.

After the 3 February meeting, the Board again visited the site. The progress in less than a month was noticeable. Hyundai had an office on the 'island', and living accommodation for some key personnel, such as Mr. Kim who was in charge of the construction of ASRY. He almost never left the site, and his capacity for work, combined with his high spirit, was impressive. As we looked towards the mainland we could see the causeway beginning to stretch out towards the island 8 kilometres offshore. Mr. Kim promised we would be driving to ASRY from the mainland before the end of the year. (This actually occurred at the end of September.)

ASRY had two permanent Board members in Bahrain, the Chairman, Majid Al-Jishi, and the Board Secretary, Mohamed Al-Khatib, then in his twenties. The latter was a Jordanian by birth and had come to Bahrain when his father, an army officer, took refuge together with his wife and four children following the Palestinian West Bank uprisings. Mohamed was of an exceptional brightness and completely bilingual in English and Arabic, with a work capacity similar to that of Mr. Kim.

My return to London on 5 February was via Beirut, where I had a meeting with Dr. Taher, who wanted news of ASRY. Petromin had an office on the 12th floor of the Holiday Inn complex which comprised hotel and office block. Dr. Taher informed me that he had recently signed a contract with our old friend, Norman Thompson, just before he left Cunard, for the management of two Petromin tankers bringing crude oil from Ras Tanura to the Jeddah Refinery on the Red Sea. We lunched together at the Yerezeldan, located on the Bay of Pigeons waterfront. I mentioned that Yousuf wanted ASRY to take a stand at the Middle East Expo in Beirut scheduled for May. Dr. Taher remarked that he hoped there would still be a peaceful city at that time as matters were becoming extremely critical, with the PLO agitating within the various refugee camps on the outskirts of Beirut.

I flew back to London the next day, 7 February. Our European agents were located in London, Paris, Genoa, Athens, Monte Carlo, Madrid (the son of Don Fernando Azqueta), Oslo, Stockholm, Copenhagen, Hamburg and Rotterdam. They were selected on the basis of not representing any shipyards which could be competitive to ASRY, while at the same time being known to VLCC shipowners. Mike and I visited each at least twice during the year to learn the views of owners in their area, in order to aim our marketing to their requirements. We both travelled a lot during 1975, which involved longer flights in the autumn, when we met with our agents in Tokyo, Hong Kong, Bombay, New York and San Francisco. Mike was good at organizing art work for ASRY's various advertisements, and a brochure was prepared during April. The 5,000 copies were soon distributed by agents, ASRY and ASRYMAR, and it became necessary to reprint in September. There were two more ASRY Board Meetings in Bahrain, one held in Lausanne at the headquarters of Navelink, Lisnave's operating company dealing with ASRY, and the sixth and last of the year in London.

Mike and I flew to Beirut in May to organize the ASRY stand for the Middle East Expo which opened on 17 May. We took the ASRY model which had been made for the cornerstone-laying ceremony in Bahrain the previous December. There were photographs of ASRY in construction, brochures, and a knowledgeable, willing Mike, sitting on the stand, ready to talk to anyone about VLCC repairing, or give them a drink of orange juice. It made a modest show and was dwarfed by our neighbours, all of whom were pushing military hardware – aircraft, tanks, guns, rockets, etc. It seemed that, apart from construction companies, ours was the only peaceful stand. All of the Gulf States were buying weaponry for national defence, and every big manufacturer was represented to display their goods (or bads!) before a hungry market. Significantly, the shooting had started, and from within the exhibition hall in the Phoenicia Hotel, we could hear mortar and machine gun fire, still contained some miles from the waterfront and the big international hotels. Before the end of the year, that area would become engulfed.

When the Exposition closed three days later, Mike and I took a taxi to Beirut Airport. *En route* one passes the largest of the refugee settlements. We saw men (not in uniform) carrying rifles and submachine guns. There were also numerous soldiers in uniform. An awkward few minutes were passed when the taxi stopped in a traffic jam alongside a young man standing on the sidewalk wearing a T-shirt and jeans, cradling a machine gun. He kept looking at us in the cab and we didn't think his expression was friendly. Fortunately, the taxi soon moved off and we reached the airport, around which there was a heavy military guard. Mike headed for London and I for Bahrain.

That May 1975 was my last visit to Beirut. The subsequent years did much to destroy that beautiful city which, since Roman times, had been the showcase of the Middle East. I have seen photographs of the remains of familiar landmarks and streets and it astonishes me that anyone still lives there in quite a normal way. Yet I have been told by Lebanese friends that there are sections of the city where life continues almost normally, with all sorts of merchandise, clothing and consumer durable shops and restaurants doing business. There are even motor car showrooms which still sell new German and Japanese cars.

In Bahrain Majid Al-Jishi, Mr. Perestrello and I had a meeting to review progress on and off site. Majid said that Hyundai were well on schedule. Manuel Perestrello and I flew back direct to London the next day, over-flying Beirut. Mr. Kawakami was in London and we had a friendly lunch. He offered KHI's help if needed on turbines – it felt as though we were back where we had been in 1970. I still correspond with Mr. Kawakami 18 years later. He remains the Japanese with whom a westerner feels no barriers of communication. There must be many others as gifted as he is in transcending such a great cultural divide, but I have never met them.

The balance of 1975 and all of 1976 were very busy times for all those involved in completing ASRY. Lisnave, through its subsidiary, Navelink, headed by Mr. Carreira and based in Lausanne (because of easier communications) was determined that ASRY would benefit from Lisnave's mistakes, and tried to avoid their earlier errors in design. Mr. Carreira achieved his aim and ASRY, in many ways, was an improvement over Lisnave. Hyundai forged ahead and the yard was rapidly taking shape.

By the end of 1976 the ASRY training school was in operation and more than 100 young Arab nationals had been trained as welders. ASRY's workforce was growing, and accommodation for expatriates had been erected. Co-operation was at a high level between all groups – for some never-defined reason, ASRY had not become just another industrial venture – instead it seemed to be handled with tender care by all of the contractors, who appeared to believe they had been entrusted to create a reality from a dream.

# 15

# JANUARY – DECEMBER 1977

ASRYMAR was very conscious that it must find a VLCC shipowner who would be willing to be the first to put his ship in an untried facility, otherwise the Arab sponsors and investors would have been grossly misled. By 1976 there had been complete market penetration, and no company operating a large tanker from 100,000 DWT upwards was unaware of ASRY. They had all been visited several times, had received ASRYMAR's direct mail correspondence with special reference to their ships, etc. All that activity, which was challenging and necessary, would not make very interesting reading a dozen or more years later, but at the time everyone's commitment was unusual and nothing in the many large projects that blossomed in the area in subsequent years can compare with the missionary zeal of our marketing of ASRY.

At ASRY Board Meetings at the beginning of 1977, members frequently asked whether we would find a ship for the inaugural ceremony, which had been scheduled for 15 December. The answer had to be 'yes', but we were still fishing for the first nibble. ASRY agents were sending monthly reports on their area's ship-owners, and forecasting vessel movements which would place them near the yard in mid-December. By the beginning of July, the familiar ship-owner reluctance was echoed, with so many repeating the same phrases about not wanting to be the guinea pig. Marine superintendents were fearful of their job if anything went wrong. There was some risk of a calamity occurring with a first docking. However, the risk was very small, especially as the docking would be under the control of one of Lisnave's most experienced dock masters.

By September ASRY had been completed. Hyundai were three months ahead of schedule. The dry dock had been tested several times, and the dock gate functioned perfectly. At the September Board Meeting, ASRY authorized offering the first docking free of cost to any VLCC prepared to be the inaugural ship to dock. ASRYMAR opposed this suggestion, maintaining it would not be necessary. The Board was becoming very uneasy, dreading the consequence of 15 December arriving, with Ministers of all the OAPEC investing states present at an empty ceremony, or at least an empty dock.

On 3 October our Italian agent telephoned to ask if I would come to Genoa and meet with the Managing Director of the Camelli Group, owners of several VLCCs. Our agent, Alberto Dallari, assured me that the company was very interested in dry docking and repairing one of their VLCCs. The next day in Genoa, Mr. Marchesani, the Managing Director of Camelli, explained that their 245,000 DWT *Ambrosiana* was headed for the Gulf. He was prepared to have it dock at ASRY, but could not wait until 15 December, as the ship would arrive off Bahrain around 21 October. He gave me the repair list and asked for a quotation. I promised an answer about the pre-inaugural date docking and the repair price the next morning.

I telexed ASRY the repair specification, advising that I would telephone the General Manager, Mr. Antonio Machado Lopes, at his home around 19:00 Bahrain time to give him an opportunity to consider the repair list. When I telephoned, I was given a repair price which I feared was high, but he confirmed that he had spoken with the Chairman who agreed that ASRY could take the *Ambrosiana* around 21 October. On 5 October Mr. Marchesani accepted the ASRY offer and confirmed that the vessel would be at ASRY, ready to dock, on 22–23 October. This was good news. There would be a very full shipping press coverage of the first docking, and others would surely follow as the guinea pig syndrome would have disappeared.

On 14 October I flew to Bahrain. It was the intention to publicize the docking widely. Of course, that could act against ASRY if anything went wrong, but we were all confident that it would be a perfect docking. Alberto Dallari and Mario Marchesani were attending, as well as members of the press, some from the USA and Japan, and of course the ASRY Board members were also present. The *Ambrosiana* arrived on the night of 22 October. About 6:00 on the morning of the 23rd, Messrs. Marchesani, Dallari and I left the Hilton Hotel by taxi. We sat on the wide back seat of the Chevrolet car, with the driver belting through the empty streets, past the airport and on to the newly finished causeway for the straight run to the ASRY gatehouse. Suddenly, Mr. Dallari looked up and screamed – a few feet in front of us was a barrier with the gatepost down, very like a closed railway crossing. The driver must have been sleepy, or intrigued by the road ahead, but he reacted quickly, braked, and the car skidded off the road on to the surrounding sand, rocked ominously, but didn't turn over. If Mr. Dallari hadn't alerted the driver by screaming, we might all have been decapitated, as the pole was at windscreen height! We got out of the car as it was stuck in the sand, and after several unsuccessful attempts to get it free, we abandoned it, walking to the road to hitch a ride on one of the ASRY buses which were bringing in some of the morning shift.

It was a clear, sunny day, with low humidity, the temperature at 21°C. The *Ambrosiana* was being manœuvred by the ASRY tugs towards the mouth of the dry dock. The gate had been opened and tugs neatly escorted the vessel into dock. When the ship was half way in, the tugs on either side backed out of the dock because, by that time, the bow cable had been attached and the powerful winch at the head of the dock pulled the *Ambrosiana* the rest of the way.

So far it had been a textbook docking. The next phase was to pump the water out of the dock and permit the *Ambrosiana* slowly to settle on to the keel blocks, which had been adjusted to her hull conformity. This would take about three hours. Mr. Marchesani wanted to go on board the ship, but it was sitting too high for access by the accommodation ladder. Mr. Carreira suggested we could get into the steel basket and the crane would lift us from the dock side on to the deck. Messrs. Carreira, Marchesani, Dallari and I got into an open steel box and were hoisted high into the air. There was a wind blowing which rocked us alarmingly and, for the second time that day, I felt my life was at risk. However, the crane driver had a very sure touch of his controls and lowered us very gently on to the *Ambrosiana* deck. The captain invited us to lunch. We sat down to a very good Italian meal, complete with two qualities of Italian wine. I was surprised to find that we were served by stewardesses instead of the usual male messroom staff, and Mr. Marchesani told us there were eight women on board, including two cooks. After lunch, the vessel was still too high to use the gangway, and we returned the same way we had come, but it seemed less hair-raising the second time.

That night the Chairman gave a large celebration party at which all the Board members attended, together with ASRY Divisional Managers, Lisnave, Navelink, press and myself. Everyone was pleased to have succeeded in putting ASRY competently to the task for which it was created.

The following morning I flew back to London loaded with still photographs and reels of film footage. A complete set of all the stills was sent to each agent so that they could be shown to shipowners in their area. Viznews added the docking instalment to the ASRY film from the footage I had brought from Bahrain. This was soon in ASRY agents' possession and they took their portable videos around to shipowners' offices to show the *Ambrosiana* docking.

The following week, agents began telexing docking requirements for vessels wishing to enter ASRY in November. Five VLCCs, two operated from Greece, one from Norway, one from France and one from England, had to be turned down because the ASRY Chairman and Board did not want to take any further ships before the inauguration ceremony, lest the inaugural docking appeared anticlimatic. The date of the ceremony could not be moved as it was intended to coincide with Bahrain's National Day, which takes place on 15 December.

This now gave ASRYMAR time to try and find a vessel from amongst the oil companies. This would attract greatest benefit to ASRY, as oil company marine managers were known to be ultra-conservative and cautious. If an oil company docked one of its VLCCs at ASRY, this would be the ultimate seal of approval.

We booked the *Mobil Pride* for the inaugural dry docking, which was to be followed immediately by the *Texaco Carribean*, and then the *Esso Dalriada*. The docking programme began to fill well into March. During November, finishing touches were being made to ASRY. By 10 December, all of the painting was complete, and it looked like a shining brand new yard, which of course it was.

There were two last-minute requests made to ASRYMAR, one from Yousuf and one from Majid. Yousuf wanted me to bring down to Bahrain a fine silver ewar, from which His Highness the Ruler, Sheikh Isa, would pour holy water from the well at Zam Zam (in Saudi Arabia) into the dry dock, thus inaugurating it. Majid wanted me to find a splendid gift which the ASRY Board could present to His Highness the Ruler on the inaugural day. He asked for suggestions. I made a few which he did not consider important enough. I asked if I could telephone him in about an hour, after thinking about it. I wanted to telephone Cartier, the jewellers, to see if it was possible before making a suggestion. Cartier said it was possible under certain conditions and I telephoned Majid to ask whether he thought a solid gold model of the yard, made by Cartier, would be a suitable gift. 'That's it,' said Majid. I told him Cartier had not yet been able to calculate their price as they had not seen a photograph or drawing of the yard. Majid said it did not matter and he was sure a firm like Cartier would quote a fair price.

I went to Cartier with photographs of the yard and a layout drawing. Mr. Brown said it was impossible to work from those, at least in the given time-scale. It was then 10 November and we wanted the finished model by 7 December. Mr. Brown said that if I could deliver him a scale model in wood by early Monday morning, 14 November, Cartier would be able to meet the deadline of 7 December. Mike Ratcliffe began frantically to search for a model maker prepared to work through the weekend to make a scaled-down replica of ASRY. During that Thursday afternoon, he spoke by telephone to six, who all turned him down, and then he struck lucky. The man said he would come to the office within an hour, discuss price, and if we agreed, he would collect photographs and drawings of ASRY. He was a man in his sixties, an old school craftsman, who instilled confidence at our first meeting. We agreed a price and he promised to bring his finished work into the office at 9:00 on Monday morning.

That Monday he delivered a very good miniature of ASRY, complete with cranes and even a VLCC sitting in the dry dock. The VLCC was just a rough shape without detail, but it was to scale and could be lifted in and out of the dry dock.

I rushed over to Cartier with the wooden 15″ × 18″ model. Mr. Brown said his craftsman could work from it. We agreed to make the ship look more like a tanker and to put *Mobil Pride* on the bow. I promised to send a profile drawing of the ship to guide them. Mr. Brown suggested that ASRY and the *Mobil Pride* be in gold, and the sea with a wave effect, in silver. The silver ewar which Yousuf had requested was much easier to find and was purchased the next day.

On 28 November Jack Aguerro, Mobil's Vice President in charge of marine activities, telephoned me from New York to say he wanted to change the docking schedule for the *Mobil Pride*. He remarked that with all the press and television coverage, he did not want to have a dirty, rusty Mobil ship photographed coming into dock. Instead he proposed that the ship arrive three days earlier, be docked, scraped and cleaned, etc. and then painted, so that on the morning of 15 December, the *Mobil Pride* would be sitting in the dock immaculately painted overall, even to the funnel markings. I said it seemed like a good idea as, in any case, the guests would be sitting on a grandstand under a marquee at the head of the dock, and they would have to wait too long if they were to watch the *Mobil Pride* being towed up to the dock mouth and then winched in, but I would have to clear it with the ASRY Chairman. Majid was also in full agreement and I telephoned Jack to say we would do it his way.

Marcella and I planned to fly to Bahrain on 8 December to help with preparations for the ceremony. On 7 December I went to Cartier to look at the model. It exceeded expectation. It was a very complete miniature of ASRY in gold, with cranes, workshops, office building, entry gate and even the causeway stretching over a slightly rippling sea. The movable *Mobil Pride* looked like a VLCC and had its name on the bow. The entire model fitted into a traditional red morocco leather Cartier box, lined with velvet. Mr. Brown was very pleased that the old established Cartier could still rise to an occasion and produce quality artisanship in a short time, as they had in the reign of King Edward VII. We boarded Concorde with one large box containing the model and a smaller box with the ewar inside. In those days Concorde had a twice weekly flight to Bahrain. It was intended to extend the route to Australia, but Malaysia did not give 'over-flight' permission, and then regrettably Concorde withdrew its Bahrain service. The flying time was reduced by two hours compared to a 747. It could have been cut more, except that Concorde had to fly subsonic until it reached the coast of Yugoslavia, when throttles were pushed forward and it achieved Mach II.

We arrived in Bahrain about midnight local time. For the very first time I encountered problems with customs. I did not realize that there was a duty to be paid on all gold imports. I explained that the Cartier box contained a gift for His Highness the Ruler and would be presented to him at the ASRY ceremony the following week. The customs officer was intractable and insisted on weighing the model. I began to fret at the way this wonderful creation was being manhandled and asked him to stop and we would telephone Majid, even if it meant waking him up. We did this, and Majid spoke with the customs official, after which we were allowed to proceed to the Bahrain Hilton with the model and ewar. The next morning I took the model to Majid's office for safekeeping. He was very pleased with ASRY's gift to the Ruler. He disclosed the sad news that after the end of the year he would resign as ASRY Chairman to concentrate on his Ministry. A month previously he had been appointed Minister of Public Works and Electric Power. We would all miss him; he had led ASRY through its construction period, always calmly and patiently, solving the various problems which arose. He would have the satisfaction of completing his tenure, with ASRY carrying out several dockings before the end of the year. He left behind Mohamed Al-Khatib to assist the new Chairman, Sheikh Khalifa Al-Khalifa. Sheikh Khalifa was a 'royal', being a cousin of the Ruler. He too became a competent Chairman, being business trained rather than engineering oriented. He had an MBA from an American University. He remained for three years until he too became a Minister – the Minister of Labour.

Bahrain was in a very festive mood. For the three evenings prior to the inaugural ceremony, cocktail and dinner parties for more than 100 guests took place. One was given by Jose Manuel de Mello, one by Yousuf's Ministry, and another by ASRY. Guests began arriving from abroad on 13 December. These included the Chairman of Lloyd's, ship-owners, bankers, oil company executives, journalists, and a number of economists from that section of the shipping and petroleum press. We had an unexpected guest in the person of Thor Heyerdahl who had some weeks previously attempted to simulate the means of travel of 3rd millennium BC emigrants who set out from the Sumerian ports at the head of the Shatt Al-Arab river and were carried into the Gulf and eventually to the Indian subcontinent. He built a boat of papyrus reeds named the *Ra*, but it began to founder just off Bahrain and a tug from ASRY went out to rescue him and his crew. They towed the *Ra* into ASRY where repairs were made, although the yard was not specialized in treating such light materials as papyrus.

All of the Bahraini notables were invited to the parties and some of these amongst the merchant families, such as the Kanoos, greatly enhanced the enjoyment of the visitors with stories of early commerce in Bahrain, which consisted mostly of pearl diving. All female guests received a pearl necklace as a memento of Bahrain.

On the morning of the great day, which dawned clear, sunny and mild, buses took the guests from the Hilton and Gulf Hotels across the causeway to ASRY. On top of the gatehouse, flags of many nations flew. By 10:00 everyone was seated on the large stand under its multi-coloured canopy which shielded the spectators from the sun. The stand was located about 50 metres from the head of the dock. In the dock, which was completely dry, rested the shining black hull and gleaming white superstructure of the *Mobil Pride*. The ship was smartly dressed in all her flags, the bow with her name towered above the dock and over the viewing stand. As the guests waited, the Bahrain National Band, dressed like British Grenadier guard bandsmen, played lively airs.

Suddenly, the sirens of the motorcycle outriders were heard, and the Ruler's car arrived, from which he and his brother, the Prime Minister, descended. In the next car were Sheikh Yamani and the Secretary General of OAPEC, Dr. Ali Al-Attiga. Descending from the cavalcade of cars were Ministers and members of the ruling families of neighbouring states. When His Highness Sheikh Isa was seated, Majid Al-Jishi approached him and placed the gold ASRY model on the table in front of his sofa. I was watching and saw the genuine surprise and pleasure registered on his face. The photographers and television crew got some excellent shots, and that night around the world, the gold model in its Cartier box was shown on television. Mr. Brown told me he had seen the coverage and that the announcer had mentioned that the model had been made by Cartier – very gratifying, unsolicited publicity.

Speeches followed, one by Majid Al-Jishi and another by Ali Al-Attiga, and finally, a poem composed for the occasion by Bahrain's poet laureate. Then the Ruler, accompanied by members of his family and the OAPEC Ministers, walked to the head of the dock, where he was handed the silver ewer containing the holy water from the well at Zam Zam. The Ruler intoned some words in Arabic and poured the water into the empty dry dock. Immediately after, the *Mobil Pride* gave three mighty blasts on her horn and the band struck up the National Anthem. The pumps then began to fill up the dock with water from the Arabian Gulf which mixed with that of Zam Zam. By evening the *Mobil Pride* was gone, and the *Texaco Carribean* had entered the dock.

After a reception at the Ruler's Palace, the ceremonies were over and ASRY had been launched on an active life.

# EPILOGUE

In the years that followed, ASRY's utilization ran at over 85 per cent while the average employment of VLCC docks around the world was 65 per cent. This was largely due to its good 'market oriented' location, effective marketing, and acceptable standards of repairs performed.

Arabization took place rapidly, and soon 80 per cent of the workforce were Arab Nationals. Divisional management had also been assumed by Arabs in the Financial, Commercial, Personnel and Production Divisions.

More than a dozen years after the inaugural docking of the *Mobil Pride*, I recall the Arabian adventure, and specifically how it all hung on such a tenuous thread. There were two events without which there would have been no ASRY. The first was the closing of the Suez Canal in 1967, which provoked the building of VLCCs, and the second was in 1973 when the 'Yom Kippur' – Arab-Israeli conflict – led to the price of oil leaping skyward. The construction cost of ASRY became insignificant when measured in the new wealth of the OAPEC states.

Nevertheless, it remains remarkable that the OAPEC states jointly agreed to invest in ASRY. It was the only industrial venture on which they did embark, although many less complicated proposals were submitted for their consideration. It must have been that the timing was propitious, and, above all, OAPEC members could not ignore the recommendations of Sheikh Yamani, whose efforts had contributed so largely to the increase in their annual national revenue. It has been most gratifying to me, having pushed the concept of ASRY past so many obstacles to the notice of Sheikh Yamani, that ASRY has justified his support of the project.